NOT LITERARY

NOT LITERARY

AURIANE DE RUDDER

Auriane de Rudder

CONTENTS

I had fun writing these. I hope you have fun reading them.

-A

1

The Literal Other Side of the Tracks

We all know being a teenager sucks, but did you know turning 18 sucks, too? Yeah. It's super lame.

When I turned 18, I thought fireworks would go off in the sky. 'Adult at Last,' they would spell as sparks rained down around me. I could finally do whatever the hell I wanted. Free from the shackles of my girl-gone-wrong suburban upbringing an—*ugh*--parents, I would be worldly, wise and mature. I would travel. I would read books that weren't assigned in school. I would have sex with people I really wanted to *and* I'd have orgasms.

But then, like...no fireworks went off. There wasn't an Auriane Liberation parade. Two months went by after my birthday and I hadn't traveled, read anything good or fucked anyone. 18 was just like 17, and 16 and 15. I was stuck. In Columbia, Maryland of all places. Built by a guy who was best known for creating most of the country's shopping malls, Columbia was basically a very mall-like experience. I felt *so* eternally high school, and I hated it.

I needed to make a change, and so I did what any girl in

my position would do. First, I dyed my blonde hair black. That was a dramatic scratch to my itch and actually suited me. Then, I booked a flight to a place I'd never been. I didn't have much money, but I scraped together what I had and placed my bet on a trip to... Tucson, Arizona.

Look, I *know*. No offense to Tucson, but it's not exactly the land of great opportunity and adventure. But I had friends there. Near, dear friends. Also, friends who wouldn't charge me to stay with them. On a limited budget, I was doing my best. Besides, Ben and Catie are a blast.

Catie and I met in the sixth grade. I was in a particularly bad mood and sat across from Catie in the cafeteria of Wilde Lake Middle. I placed my tray with Elios pizza and French fries with runny ranch dressing in front of me. I put my four quarters—for 'snack'—on the table in a little pile next to my tray. I bit into my soggy pizza.

I don't remember exactly what Catie said, but I do remember her laugh. It was taunting and high pitched. Like a cross between a baby-doll with a pull-string and a hyena.

She laughed, "Ahahahahahahah!" and flicked one of my quarters off of the table and onto the speckled tile floor.

This bitch.

"Catie, stop," I told her, not in the mood.

She laughed, "Ahahahahahahah!" and then she did it again; She flung another one of my quarters right off the side of the table.

"Catie, STOP IT," I said.

"Ahahahahahahah!" and wouldn't you know, she did it again.

Look. I'm a reasonable person. There isn't really anything you can do to make me hit you. Except that. Repetition drives me nuts. If someone does something annoying three times—and yes, situations like this have happened other times with similar results—I just SNAP.

I wanted to slap her, but it just so happened that I was holding onto a piece of pizza in my slappin' hand. So, I shoved that hot Elios right in Catie's face. Smooooosh. Take that. I blacked out after that and don't remember what happened next, but I do know that Catie and I became, like, best friends. Middle school girls are weird like that.

Ben and I don't have a rage-blackout meetcute. But, fittingly enough, we met through Catie a few years later. The three of us got along famously. So, when I found out Catie and Ben were living together in Tucson, it was a no-brainer. I packed a few outfits, bought a disposable camera and was on my way.

Once I had arrived, our days consisted mostly of thrift store shopping, smoking weed and going to the nearby Mexican drive thru for Horchata and tacos. It wasn't boring, because Ben and Catie are both wildly hilarious, but it wasn't the Adult Adventure I was looking for, either.

"Is there, like, anything I should see while I'm here?" I asked Catie one late afternoon as I passed her the blunt.

"I mean...it's, like, a normal place, you know?" Catie said as she exhaled a long plume of weed smoke, "There's, like, college bars we could go to."

"Yeah, but I don't have an ID," I told her.

"I know, me either," she said.

This was funny, because as teenagers, we all had IDs that got us into raves that were 18 and up. Now that we were 18, we needed to be 21. Bars were the next becoming-an-adult frontier. Like I said. 18 sucks.

"We could take her to Mexico," Ben offered, taking the blunt from Catie and joining in the rotation, "You don't need an ID to drink in Mexico."

"How far is Mexico?" I asked.

"Not far. Like less than two hours," Catie said, "Shit, we can go tonight if you want to," she added and passed me the blunt.

I sucked in another gulp of pot smoke, holding it in my lungs. I extinguished the blunt on the bottom of my shoe and let out a whoosh of an exhale.

"Hey! What the fuck, I wasn't done with that!" Catie said.

"You're driving," I told her.

***

We packed the car with a few of Catie's friends--Alice a blonde haired, blue eyed BBW with a thick German accent and her gay sidekick Michael shared the front passenger seat. Ben and I smooshed ourselves into the back with Marisa and Angela, two super cute Mexican stoner girls. We headed south, blasting Cumbia from the half- blown speakers of Catie's Volvo.

"Yo, Alice, pass that back here," Marisa asked as Alice took a sip of MadDog 2020.

Marisa lit a joint in the back seat.

"I'll trade you, dude," Marisa spoke like a feminized Tommy Chong, all stoney baloney.

"Nah, don't give her that," Angela said, "She's too crazy when she's cross faded," Angela had a sweet voice and a slight Mexican accent.

"Pssh whatever, girl, takes one to know one," Marisa said as Angela took the MadDog from Alice and swallowed a gulp.

We were about 30 minutes from our destination, and everyone was smoking what they had to smoke, and sipping what they had to sip. You know, pregaming. We passed around joints and bottles until we got close enough to the border to see patrol cars. Catie sprayed cherry air freshener into the vents and blasted the AC to de-weed-smoke the car. Alice and Michael coughed, half from the weed and half from the sticky sweet smell.

The border was unremarkable. A single green highway sign labeled BORDER CROSSING TO MEXICO ONLY directed cars in one direction. Catie pulled into an adjacent dirt parking lot just before the exit. There were a handful of border cops throughout the lot.

We left the car and hoofed it toward the dusty, pedestrian entrance.

"Alright everybody...be cool," Michael said, stoned and laughing, as we passed by a group of officers.

The sun was just starting to set, lowering behind a few cash exchange shops marked PESOS along the way.

"Don't worry, everyone here will take American cash," Catie told us as we walked, our leader, "Plus everything is, like, a dollar. It's awesome."

We took a few steps and Catie stopped abruptly.

"Does anyone have weed on them?" She asked before we entered the customs line.

"All clear," Ben said.

"Not on me," I replied.

"Nah dude, I left it in the car," Marisa chimed in.

"Don't look at me, I'm the innocent one," Angela added, her eyes a hot shade of red.

"Riiiight," Catie said, laughing.

"For real, I'm not even crazy in Mexico. They'll arrest you here so fast," Angela said.

Alice and Michael's eyes widened as Michael tossed a half a joint out of his pocket and left it in the dirt. He smiled and shrugged.

"It's cool, there's more in the car for later," he said.

"Word, cuz' they'll take it if you have it on you," Catie said as she led us into the line, "Or arrest you and make you pay them all your money if you act like a dick. That shit really sucks."

Now, maybe you've been to Mexico before. Maybe not. Mexico is a huge, diverse country with loads of different experiences to be had. You can go do yoga with hippies in Tulum or you can dance the night away in Mexico City. You can dive the Cenotes in the Riviera Maya or you can avoid the cartel in Sinaloa. You can peruse unique shops in Baja or you can go to a seedy strip club in Nogales. We were in Nogales, so we chose to go to a seedy strip club. Well, two.

The first strip club was, much like the dirt parking lot and customs line, unremarkable. It was a small, dark room with cigarette smoke in the air. A fat man in silver tipped cowboy boots escorted us in, and sat us at the precipice of the stage.

"Two drinks each," he said in perfect English.

"Hola. Tequila, por favor," I said, proud of myself like an idiot.

We sat, waiting for the show to begin as the man ducked behind an adjacent counter top to pour our tequila. More Cumbia began to play and a single bare bulb flickered on above the stage. An overweight stripper walked toward us slowly, barefoot, in a neon pink string bikini. Behind her, another girl was curled up in the corner. She was either sleeping, passed out, or dead, we couldn't be sure.

"Jesus, this is bleak," I said to Angela and Marisa, who were sitting almost in each other's laps, nervously observing this mess.

"No, I don't like this at all," Angela said, leaning away from the stage and even closer to Marisa.

The bouncer put two shots of tequila in front of each of us. I slammed both immediately and gestured for our friends to follow suit. I passed the bouncer a twenty-dollar bill. I would have asked for change, but he startled me by yelling toward the stage.

"Levantate! Piche puta, levantate!" He stomped over to the sleeping stripper on stage and kicked her, hard, in the ribs.

"Ayeeee," she groaned and stirred. At least she wasn't dead.

"What the fuck," Michael said and slammed his two shots of tequila, "We need to go."

"Thees is, like, illegal, yah? Like, abuse?" Alice said in her thick German accent.

"It's not cute, that's for sure," Ben said.

Angela had buried her head into Marisa's shoulder, unable to look as the man kicked the girl again, not as hard this time, but still. *No.* We stared.

"Dude, that's enough. Let's get the fuck out of here," Marisa said, pushing Angela off her lap.

Angela downed her tequila and nodded toward the exit, "Let's go, please," she pleaded, but we were already walking toward the door.

"I know where we should go," Catie said, still optimistic.

I kept my head down and stared at the fat man's cowboy boots as we left, holding my breath. We rushed across the street and away from the bar faster than I could say 'Cambio, por favor.'

"Okay, we literally need to cross the train tracks and there's a really good strip club," Catie said, leading us across some neglected tracks and over a dusty stretch of land.

I don't know why we were so into strip clubs, maybe the tawdry nature of it was a draw, I'm not sure. Whatever the motivation, the next club *delivered*.

Lord Black's was a huge establishment. We walked into the converted warehouse building and immediately were transported to a fantasy world. American music thumped throughout, and pink and yellow lights shone over four stages packed with beautiful strippers in clear, plastic heels. These girls were pretty and downright athletic. I watched as one woman climbed to the top of a pole and artfully flipped and twirled her way back down, simultaneously taking off her top. She landed delicately at the base of the pole and threw her legs open into a center split, her labia about three inches from a patron's face.

"This is like a movie!" I said, in awe.

"Whoa," Angela said, still clinging onto Marisa.

"These bitches are hot," Marisa added.

We slowly made our way to some available seats and all watched, in awe.

"I told you this place is the bomb," Catie said, nudging me and Ben.

"We need drinks," I told her, smiling at a dancer on stage as she crawled toward us on her hands and knees.

"Whoa!" Ben yelled as she rolled onto her back slammed her high heels together, hard, making a loud CLACK! "She *scared* me," he said, delighted, and giggled.

"Hola guapo," She said as she rolled onto her stomach, looking toward Ben and Michael, "You wanna lap dance baby?" She asked, perhaps unaware they were totally gay.

"Maybe later," Ben yelled over the music.

"We need drinks," I said, again, to no one in particular.

"You want to drink for free?" A man's deep voice came from behind me.

I turned to see two bouncers, both in Lord Black's security tee shirts, standing against the wall with their arms crossed.

"Hell yeah, I wanna' drink for free," I told them.

"We want them," one of the men said, and pointed to Marisa and Angela, who were, along with the rest of my friends, completely mesmerized by the girls on stage.

"What do you mean you *want them*?" I asked.

"Just to dance. You can drink all you want for free but they have to dance," the other man told me.

Okay look. I know I'm not about to win any friend of the year awards here, but I figured why not? I honestly thought after all the free alcohol we could drink, Marisa and Angela wouldn't mind stripping. And if they did, we could just run, right? What could possibly go wrong in this nice little border town? By the end of the night everyone would probably be thanking me for saving them so many pesos.

"Okay, sure," I said to the men, "We're all drinking tequila," I added and turned back to my friends, all hypnotized by the naked dancers.

The two men high fived before heading over to the bar to get our "unlimited alcohol." I put that in quotes because, predictably, it was not, in fact, unlimited. No, amigos. Turns out it was extremely limited. These guys came back with one shot for each of us. We had barely bit into our accompanying limes before they turned to Marisa and Angela.

"Baila," one man said, and pointed at the stage.

"What the fuck?" I asked, "Whoa dude, you owe us *way* more alcohol first," I said, loud enough for everyone to hear.

"Auriane what are you talking about?" Catie asked me.

Marisa and Angela sat, wide eyed and hugging each other as the bouncers stepped closer.

"You drink, now they dance," a bouncer said, nodding to me, and then nodding to the girls.

"Ay Dios mio, no!" Angela looked genuinely horrified as the bouncer put an unfriendly hand on her shoulder.

"Auriane what in the fuck are these guys talking about?" Catie asked, pissed.

"Okay," I said, turning to Angela, lowering my voice, "So I think I kinda' fucked up," I pulled Catie in close, and huddled with the girls, "I think I kinda' sold you to these guys for shots. But listen, you just have to dance--"

"What the fuck!?" Marisa whispered, "How many shots?"

"Ay Dios mio," Angela said, signing a holy trinity on her chest, "I am a CAT-O-LIC!" She yelled out.

A security guard pulled Angela out of her seat by the arm.

"Don't fuckin' touch her," Marisa stood and positioned herself between the guard and Angela, "I'll just pay for the shots. Yo pago, si?"

Marisa pulled out a 20-dollar bill and offered it to the man holding Angela. He took it and put it in his pocket. The second security guard then put his arm on Marisa's shoulder, firmly. He smiled and nodded toward the stage. Marisa's face dropped. She shook the man off her shoulder and turned to me.

"Okay. Looks like we are gonna' dance," she said, taking a shot off the bar and slamming it back, "But you're coming with us," she said to me as she wiped tequila off her chin.

"Right. We'll all do it," I said looking at Catie and nodding, "We'll do it together, right? It'll be fast and easy." I told her, "Alice do you want to come?" So far, she hadn't been dragged into this.

"I'll paass on dat, but you girls haave fun," she said, sipping on her 'free' tequila as both security guards pushed the four of us toward the entrance to the stage.

"Ay Dios mio," Angela said again, tears in her eyes, "I'm not a stripper..." her voice trailed off, "I'm not a stripper, I'm a CAT-O-LIC!" she pleaded one last time.

"Fuck it," Marisa said, "We got this," she said to Angela.

Catie pulled back a thick velvet curtain at the edge of the stage and took a few steps forward. I pulled her back, behind the curtain and leaned in to the other girls.

"Okay listen, we gotta' do this quick. No one take off your pants, tops only, okay? Me and Catie will go to the edge of the stage and, like, touch each other's titties. Marisa you take the right side of the stage, Angela, take the pole on the end. Do a few turns, take off your shirts and then sexy walk back and we are DONE, you got it?" It was like a fucked-up sports huddle, like we were discussing a football play.

We stepped out on stage, all of us visibly shaken. Bathed in pink stage light, we waited in silence for what felt like an eternity, but was actually about a half a second. Then the music started.

"My neck...."

Angela wrapped her hands around the pole.

"My back..."

Catie and I walked—trying to be sexy, but also keep in mind we were both wearing jeans at the time—to the center of the stage.

"Lick my pussy and my crack..." of course *this* would be the song we have to strip to.

Marisa was the first to take off her tank top, then Catie, Angela and I followed, one by one, trying to strip as little as possible and run out the three-minute song. Things were actually going well, everyone was sticking to the 'plan' and no one had gotten very naked. For just a moment it was pretty fun.

"My neck..." the blinding pink light shifted out of my eyes and over the crowd.

"My back..." it was then that I realized we were in trouble.

Remember how earlier I thought this place was like a movie? Okay, well if this was a movie, this next shit would have been shot in slow motion.

I saw, in the center of the club, a handful of dancers had abandoned their stages and were huddled, like our rival sports team, staring at us on stage. It wasn't a half a second later that the huddle broke, and the girls started *running* at us. They legit *RAN*. Their huge high heels clomped like horses' hooves over the floor and they bounded at us, leaping onto the stage and tearing at our clothing. These bitches ripped all of our clothes off, piece by piece. I am not exaggerating when I tell you they ripped Catie's jeans in fucking half. This terrifying, hot woman just pulled them right off her body in one, savage tug!

"Por favor, mi gato es feo!" I begged one of the dancers as she ripped my pants off, snarling at me, "Periodo! Periodo!" I shouted.

I thought if I told her I had my period she might let me keep my panties on. And whattayaknow, she did! My bra and my pants, on the other hand, she tore to shreds. I was too busy to see as far as Marisa and Angela at the end of the stage, but figured they were receiving the same treatment. The crowd roared as the girls attacked us, saliva dripping off their teeth as they laughed and laughed and laughed. And then...they stopped.

The song came to an end, thank God, and the dancers retreated, still laughing and picking scraps of torn fabric out of their acrylic fingernails. I bent down to pick up my tattered clothes, as Catie did the same. My bra was hanging off the end of the stage, frightening close to an old, fat man with a greasy comb-over. As I bent over to retrieve it, he pinched my nipple, hard, and smiled.

"Yucky," I said and shook him off of me, shuddering.

I walked backstage, utterly defeated, picking up more scraps of our clothing on my way.

Backstage, Marisa and Catie were sorting our torn panties and bras. I added the scraps I had collected to the pile. Marisa picked up Angela's green pair of panties.

"Yo, where's Angela?" she asked, twirling the panties around on one finger.

I looked at Catie. Catie looked at Marisa. Marisa looked at me. There was a moment of silence as we inched back over to the edge of the stage. The bass-heavy music started up again as Catie pulled back the velvet curtain. The three of us stood, half hidden as we stared. We watched as the pink lights came back around and focused on Angela, now butt ass naked and freely twirling around the pole. Men threw pesos at her as she arched her back and smiled. She moved with ease as she stood and did a slow and sexy body roll. She positioned a leg against the pole and slowly slid a finger inside herself.

"Dude," Marisa said.

"Duuude," Catie said.

"...Ay..Dios mio," I whispered.

2

Babycorn

The year was 2004. GW had just won his second term as US president, and I was but a babe enrolled at the University of Baltimore. It was fall. The leaves on the trees in Mount Vernon softened the blow of another 4-year term with stuttering Stanley; the red, yellow and orange creating a comforting glow. That day, I had a philosophy paper due. I did not have a printer. I tossed on a loose sweater and capri pants and put a leash on my dog, Sinatra.

"What did you get into?" I asked him, wiping some muck from his muzzle.

I looked into the kitchen and saw that the dog had helped himself to some leftover Chinese takeout, salvaged from the trashcan, now lying on its side. Messy, but also an impressive feat for my little five-lb Chihuahua.

"Sinatraaaa," I shook my finger at him and dropped the leash.

I did a half-assed clean-up of the kitchen floor, muttering curse words under my breath. It was hot in the apartment. The landlord had already turned on our radiator heat and despite all of my open windows, I was sweating through my shirt.

"Fuck it," I said, wiping sweat from my brow, and left the mess.

I picked up Sinatra's leash and headed out for the University library. It was an Indian Summer, wait—Native American Summer? Anyway, it was unseasonably warm for Baltimore in November.

Now look. These were different times. Victoria's Secret was just *what you wore* if you were a middle-class college girl. The VS catalog was a sick source of inspiration arriving in my family's mailbox each month since my adolescence. The magazine (now defunct thank God) was an airbrushed barrage of wildly thin and beautiful women, mostly in lingerie. The catalog shaped my ideals about how I should look as a young woman. Of course, I didn't look like any of the models in those pages. None of us did. I *could,* however, wear and purchase what they were wearing. At the end of summer in 2004? They were wearing platform flip flops.

So, the heat in the apartment. The heat outside. The misogynistic ideal of what a woman should look like brought on by tacky marketing of underwear? Yeah. They were all factors at play here. I set off in my stupid platform flip flops, only a few blocks from the University of Baltimore Computer Lab.

As I hurried up Charles Street, passing restaurants and shops, stopping to let Sinatra pee on a lamp post or three, one the platform flip flops snapped. The piece holding my foot to the shoe flung out from in between my toes, and sent my right foot careening into an uneven block of city sidewalk.

"Fuck!" I yelled out, tripping over myself, "Achh," I looked down to see a large chunk of my big toe was hanging there, loosely.

Blood gushed onto the pavement. I checked my phone. It was 2:42. My paper was due by 3. It was written, but I needed to print it and get it into the hands of my professor, two buildings over from the lab.

"Fuck!" I said again. A passing hobo looked at my bloody stump and recoiled.

Thank the angels, because I was right across the street from my work, Liam's Pint-Sized Pub. I hurried over to the tiny bar, and pushed through the front door. Liam was there, tinkering with our line system, one thing on a list of many that needed to be tinkered with.

"Hey Liam!" I chirped. I really liked my boss.

"Ah, hey Auriane what's up?" Liam responded in his light Irish accent, tipping his flat top cap.

The bar wasn't open yet and Liam seemed sleepy, but was more likely hungover. We drank a lot during the Bush Administration.

"Do you have a first aid kit here? I sliced my foot open and I need to get to class," I told him.

Liam didn't have a first aid kit, but he had vodka and a few Band-aids, and so we made due. I still had no shoe.

"Do you have a pair of shoes?" I asked Liam. He looked down at his feet, "I mean other than your own?"

My eyes darted around the bar. There was caulk. There was booze. There was...a staple gun! I proceeded to staple my flip flop back together and after a few tugs on the adjoined strap didn't pull anything loose, I was satisfied.

"Alright, Liam thank you, thank you, thank you. I gotta' run. Can I keep this for now?" I asked, pushing the staple gun into my bag, "In case the shoe falls apart again?"

"Sure thing, see you tonight I'm sure." Liam tipped his cap again and returned to his tinkering.

I took off for the computer lab, with pep in my bloody step. I had only minutes to print out my paper and deliver it to my professor. I didn't have time for Sinatra to stop and sniff every pee spot on our way, so I scooped up his five-pound body and placed him in my purse, safely snuggled away from the staple gun. I arrived at the library winded, sweaty, and with only six minutes to spare.

I set my bag down next to a computer, logged in and hit print. I waited a moment until I heard the familiar hum of the printer starting up, and walked over to grab my pages. Sinatra, no longer content to sit in my purse, followed. After hearing some grumbles from other students, I noticed that my dog was walking around the lab. I ran after him and quickly scooped him up, holding him against my chest with one arm, my paper tucked under the other.

This is where things got yucky. The library attendant, a cute guy I had flirted with in the past, approached me.

"Hi Jay," I smiled, walking quickly back to my workspace, ready to grab my bag and get going.

"Hey, Auriane. You know...you can't have a dog in here," he said, feigning a half smile.

"Oh, sure," I said, unphased, "I'll put him back in the bag."

"No, he can't, like, be in the bag in here, either," He informed me.

"You know, he's actually a service--" I started with an eye-roll.

But then, my shoe snapped. I was sent into another stumble, letting out a string of loud, involuntary curse words.

"FuckAssShitMother!" I dropped the dog back onto the carpet.

Sinatra and I both scurried back toward my purse. I walked with my broken shoe, now loosely hanging from my ankle, muttering more curse words.

"SonofaGoddamnShittingAss."

"I just said, you cannot have dogs in the computer lab," Jay started in again, "You need to go," Jay added, proud of himself for some reason.

I sat down at the workspace and pulled the shoe off of my ankle. I looked up at Jay and glared. A few bloody Band-Aids dangled from my toe. Sinatra, standing next to my feet, started a dreaded, familiar convulsion.

"Oh shit," I said.

I dug deep in my purse. I knew what was about to happen. I pulled out a collapsible water container and popped it open. I held it under Sinatra's mouth as he started to vomit up the Chinese food he had gorged on earlier.

"Ugh, Jesus," Jay said.

"Oh, I'm sorry, it's just Chinese—" as I was trying to explain it was just Chinese food, Sinatra belched loudly.

Slowly, slithering as if it were alive, a mucous-covered baby corn from last night's fried rice writhed out of the dog's stinking mouth. Jay gasped. I gasped. Covered in mucous, the cornlette looked like a parasite from a horror movie. It was terrifying.

"You really need to go," Jay exclaimed and covered his nose and mouth in disgust.

"I am trying to go!" I told him, setting the collapsible cup of dog vom down on the desk and pulling the staple gun from my purse.

Of course, I only intended to use the gun to staple my shoe back together. But Jay thought I was an actual crazy person and wanted to staple him. He threw both arms in front of his face to shield himself.

"Please! Don't do it!" He shouted.

I just looked at him, as if he were the crazy one, and then went about stapling my shoe with a shrug. I loaded the dog into my purse and gathered my papers.

"Thank you for the printer! We'll see you soon!" I shouted out as I rushed out onto the street, carrying the cup of vomit.

Jay stood there defeated. He was angry, confused and mostly--I think—scared of me.

I still had one minute to get to my professor. I tossed the slithering babycorn in a trashcan on my way across the street, careful not to trip in those stupid Victoria's Secret flip flops.

3

Dirty Donuts

George Chapman is the fattest person I know.

He isn't the fattest person you know, but that's because you haven't gotten to know him yet. He is not wider, or mushier than many of the fat people you will encounter. He won't cramp you more than your average obese person on a Southwest flight, or—at first glance—seem any bigger than an overweight person taking up two seats on the subway. But, inside, George Chapman is the fattest of the fatty-fat-fats. He lives for food. Grease surely runs through his veins, not blood, as in you or me. He is solely motivated by food, and refuses to participate in the world we live in. Instead, George eats his way through his own edible earth; his is a world which simply orbits around his next McDonald's run.

George looks like a man living on Planet McDonald's. A younger version of Peter Parker from Family Guy, George is round in all the wrong places. His sloppily ironed white work-shirts stretch tight over his bulbous midsection. The button securing his chino pants is frequently pushed to its limit, creating a dangerous environment for all that cross his path. One day that button will pop. Someone's going to lose an eye.

He fidgets frequently. Every minute or so, George runs his hands through his hair, distributing whatever crumbs and grease were once on his fingers, to their new home on his scalp. These head-inhabitants-- depending on the time of day--may be the remnants of one of many breakfast Mc-Muffins. If it's later in the afternoon? Perhaps a Whopper. George's sandy brown hair, which is always heavily greased—not from hair product, but from fast-food prod-uct—is trumped only by his oily and broken-out skin. This results in a red, shiny quality. Like Santa's. But a super gross Santa. Like the serial-killer one in that holiday episode of Tales from the Crypt.

George, however, is no Santa. He lacks any Santa-like qual-ities. George is not generous. He will not share with you even a morsel of his plentiful breakfast, lunch or dinner. He is a hoarder of food. Or, he hoards it for the five minutes he can keep it from his mouth. But not only does George eat all the food he can get his saturated sausage-y fingers on, oh no. In its absence, George talks about food. Constantly. It's as if he can't talk about anything else.

George and I met while we were working for Clarity, a small staffing firm in downtown Chicago. A start-up lead by eager young professionals, our bosses were always trying to bolster our come-up efforts. Part of this bolstering meant that George and I were asked to attend a seminar intended to 'fur-ther our technical knowledge in an ever-changing market.' Whatever. The pay-off was that if we went to the seminar, we both got a raise. I promptly booked us two seats, although the next available slots were for well over a month later.

"George, will February third and fourth work for you for the conference? I know it's forever from now but that's the earliest pair of spots I could find," I asked.

I stood over George's cubicle, surveying that morning's crumpled sheets of yellow McDonald's sandwich wrappers. I counted six for the day, so far. It was only 9 a.m.

"Sure, that's fine," George replied, "Do you think they'll be serving lunch there?" He looked up, eagerly.

"George, I—I don't know. It's more than a month away," I counted two more wrappers, hiding in his trashcan.

"Because if they're serving a hot lunch, I won't have to bring something. That's why I need to know," he said, matter-of-factly, turning back to his computer.

"I don't know, George. But I'd like to confirm our reservation, so you are available on those dates, yes?" I asked.

"Well, where is the building?" George was typing away, his fingerprints leaving greasy smudges on his keyboard as he went.

"It's downtown, George." His red, waxy face was lit like a 3D-movie in the blue hue of the computer screen.

"Well, where downtown, exactly, because if it's near any good restaurants we can just go and get lunch. That might be what we need to try and do."

"Jesus Christ, George I don't know. Can you make the seminar or not?" I stood over him.

"I guess I'll just plan to bring something, just in case," George replied, "But hopefully they'll buy us lunch."

"Oh my god. Ok George. Let's hope so," As I walked away, my high heels clicked on the linoleum floor, because, duh, George chose the cubicle next to the kitchen.

***

One bright, windy and extra-frigid morning—not at all uncommon in Chicago--I was early for work. Not only was I early, but I was feeling oddly upbeat and generous. I decided to buy breakfast for the entire office. I hurried through the icy city streets in search of the nearest donut shop.

Inside the Dunkin Donuts, I loaded up on only the best—lemon jellys, Boston cremes, and of course maple frosted—and was back on track to get to work just in time. I precariously balanced the two large boxes of donuts alongside the two jumbo brown boxes of hot coffee, carrying my own individual coffee, as well as my oversized purse and laptop. All in heels. I was a business woman about town, I was. I was on time, cheery as the day is long and looking good while I did it all. Who says you need ugly snow boots for a Chicago winter?

I arrived in front of our office at 1212 LaSalle Street ready to conquer the world. A reasonably hot guy opened the building's front door for me, seeing that my arms were full. I thanked him and stepped forward onto the slick, slate entrance. I turned back to smile at the man, but instead felt my feet slip beneath me. Oh no. Oh God. I was going down. Would I choose to toss the delicious donuts and catch myself, or smear myself across the downtown pavement and save the treats?

A rational woman would have sacrificed the donuts. She would have tossed the coffee. She would have used her arms to break her fall. In fact, a rational woman may have even sacrificed her laptop and purse, had the fall been as treacherous as mine. But at that time in my life, I was no rational woman. I clutched the coffee—both the boxed coffee and my individual one—for dear life, and hugged my body around the boxes of donuts. My laptop and purse only acted as unbalanced weight on my body, and somehow, as I coiled in to protect my goods, my feet flipped upward, as if I was levitating momentarily on a magician's table. This means that when gravity had its inevitable way with me, I landed smack down on my ass. Not just my ass, which is cushioned for a reason, but my ass-bone. Also known as the coccyx, the ass bone is one of many you really, really don't want to break.

THWACK. I laid still on the pavement. Powdered sugar floated through the air like fresh snow flakes. I was crying, involuntarily, from pain and shock. I had seriously injured myself over a few lousy donuts. Nope, I was no rational woman. I was a damn fool. I wiped at my tears from my spot on the slushy sidewalk. The hot-ish guy leaned over me. My savior.

"You just wiped chocolate on your face," he said.

Maybe not my savior.

I looked at my gloved hand, covered in a nearby smooshed donut's chocolate icing.

"Do you want me to call an ambulance?" the (slightly less-hot, now) guy asked.

"No, no. I'm okay. Just help me get up please," I said, my voice shaky.

I had a job, sure. But one thing I did not have was decent

insurance. So broken ass-bone or not, I was gonna' have to tough this one out on my own.

As the not-as-hot-guy helped me to my feet, I started to feel the severity of my injuries. Without the help of fear and shock, my ankle throbbed. Hot, sharp pain shot down my spine and seemed to divide into each leg, sending that shock to my heels and right back up to where it started, over and over. I started to cry again when I noticed the spilled coffee down my new winter coat. It was torn in two places that I could see, and my dirty donuts were scattered all over the icy ground around me. I was in pain, I looked like shit, and my donuts were covered in street grime. Not-so-hot-guy noticed my tears, and hurriedly started picking up the dirty donuts, putting them back in their original boxes. He gingerly handed me each box, along with the crushed, dripping coffee containers.

"What the fuck am I supposed to do with these?" I asked him as building security helped me limp to the elevator.

At the 14th floor, I thanked security for the escort and limped the last few steps to the office alone. The pain was excruciating, but I was hell-bent on not incurring a $5,000 visit to the E.R. I reached the front door and slowly pushed my way through.

In our lobby, our bosses were holding our morning meeting. Each staff member, dressed professionally, and ready to take on the day, stood, staring at me. Mouths were agape. Tierra, a fresh-faced recent grad who worked in the cubicle next to mine looked at me as if I had been assaulted. I looked like I had. My clothing was ripped and disheveled. I was covered in white powder. I was carrying crumpled boxes, dripping hot brown who-knows-what. The chocolate streaked across my face absolutely looked like poop.

I struggled to the nearest trashcan, and deposited the dripping coffee boxes. I then tossed the donut boxes alongside in an adjacent can and leaned against the wall of a cubicle. My breathing was slow and labored. The pain was too much.

"I got you guys donuts. But then I fell," I sighed, my voice cracking as tears continued to stream down my face.

I turned to walk to my desk, but was interrupted by Adam, the company's young CEO.

"Um, excuse me?" He asked sheepishly.

"Yes, Adam?" I turned to him, wet-eyed.

"That's the recycling bin," he pointed to the can filled with donut boxes, "Would you mind?"

I limped back over to the bin and removed the donuts. "No, not at all," I said, slamming the filthy boxes on the meeting room table, instead.

I started limping back toward my desk, breathing loudly and deliberately so as not to pass out from the pain. Fat George, this time, stopped me.

"Hey buddy!" He remarked, administering a greasy fist bump to my shoulder, nearly knocking me over again, "Are any of those donuts okay to eat?"

***

Far be it for me to let a broken ass-bone keep me from a good party. When Clarity announced that our company Christmas party was coming up, I immediately RSVP'd for two. I imagined what I would wear--my sparkly black holiday dress and matching stilettos, of course. I would bring my friend Billy, a tall and handsome confidante. Gay enough to be better dressed than anyone at the party, but seemingly straight enough to pass for a date, Billy was more than great arm candy. Billy was also kind, and had worked in nursing. This meant that he could help me limp along throughout the night, and hold me over the toilet when I had to pee. We were close, and he was compassionate. If anyone was going to see me awkwardly positioned and naked from the waist down, Billy would be best.

The event was an open-bar soiree, my favorite kind, and would also feature a swanky five-course meal. What pain I couldn't subdue with my painkillers, I figured I could subdue with alcohol. Free alcohol. I was excited, although I wondered if my coworkers would tease me for bringing a different kind of donut—the orthopedic kind—to the table.

There was a ton of food at the party. Our five dishes were unique, tasteful and very large for a multiple-course meal. We were offered option after gourmet option, including stuffed crab Portobello mushrooms, an extensive oyster sampler, lobster ceviche, some particularly delicious grilled scallops, and even a Funghi pizza. That's Fancy for 'mushroom pizza,' possibly my favorite thing after free booze. Those were just the apps, before a hearty entrée: either the black pepper and almond rubbed rack of lamb, or a flank steak with garden salad. Each item was paired with a wine selection, but we were also welcome to order cocktails. Dessert would end the feast, a selection of fruit and crème brulee tartes.

We ate, we drank. We ate more. We drank more. We drank

a lot more. Shots were served, and bellies were full. Before any of our entrees arrived, we were all stuffed to our brims. Well, almost all of us.

The tables were littered with half-eaten apps and empty wine glasses. Servers scurried to clear the uneaten items in preparation for our main course, but were met with a loud protest from—you guessed it—Fat George.

"Why would you clear those?" George interrupted a waiter, grabbing him by the arm, sweat dripping down his red, furrowed brow.

"It is time for the entrée, I'm sorry I didn't realize you were still working on this one," the waiter, a consummate professional, replied.

But George wasn't 'still working on' the appetizers. In fact, George had approached a waiter cleaning *our* table. George wasn't even sitting there. He was sharking our leftovers!

"Well, please leave the appetizers," George said firmly, "I will finish them," he said, looking pointedly at each of the tables before looking back to the waiter.

I sat, not in shock, and not surprised. Mostly, I was embarrassed. The tuxedoed waiter gave us all a look of disapproval. I felt like I should discipline George as if he were a younger brother. I did not. My butt hurt too badly to get up and I was drunk.

The appetizers were left at each table, and entrees were squeezed in every-which way by irritated servers. George and his girlfriend Patty—after devouring their entrees without so much as a breath between bites, then made their way around the dining room, picking at the remaining appetizers spread throughout. Billy and I watched in horror and amazement. The couple glided through the room like a pair of sharks. Circling and eating. Circling and eating.

At the end of the meal, the only thing that ached more than my ass was my stomach. No one sitting at our table of eight could imagine taking one more bite. I looked around to the other tables. Everyone seemed to be stuffed. Even George and Patty had finally taken a seat and seem satiated. Their sticky fingers had been licked clean, along with their silverware, and maybe even their plates. The table looked as if no one had ever sat down. George and Patricia weren't sharks. George and Patricia were vacuum cleaners.

The staff party continued, as we replaced eating with drinking. Our focus was no longer how much George could eat, but how much the rest of us could chug. The restaurant grew tired of us the more we drank, and a handful of Clarity workers—Billy and myself included—decided to continue the party at a local dive bar.

Billy helped me as I limped down the stairs of the restaurant and out onto the freezing sidewalks of Wrigleyville. We stayed a few steps behind the rest of the group, me with my inflatable donut in hand, Billy teasing me lovingly about it the entire way. We took our time, despite the cold, because we had no choice. I was mobile, but barely. We walked by the Cubs stadium, decorated for Christmas alongside many of the other businesses and storefronts. I balanced my donut on one arm, and my purse on the other. Billy wedged himself somewhere into the mix, switching sides, depending on when I winced or let out a pained cry.

The cold was unbearable, but since we were forced to walk so slowly, we tried to enjoy the walk. I looked into each shop, bar, or restaurant, trying hard to find something pretty to alleviate the sting of the weather, and the sting of my ass. I even looked into the corner McDonald's, watching people eat their McChicken sandwiches off the dollar menu, feeling slightly guilty about my expensive Christmas meal. That's when I saw it.

By golly, it was my very own Christmas Miracle. A weird and gross miracle, but a wonder, nonetheless. Sitting in plain view of us was George and his girlfriend Patty, feeding one another fast food sandwiches. *Sensually.*

I stopped to observe the erotic beasts in their natural habitat. It was if my eyes were set on zoom. I saw grotesque close-ups of George's fingers being suckled by Patty's moist lips as he fed her a sweet piece of burger bun. I watched as George wiped the remaining crumbs into his hair, and shook his head slightly, shooting Patricia his best, sexy look. I imagined I was a crumb, sitting atop George's scalp. I imagined the forest of other greasy bits, nestled in George's mop. Half hair, half McDonald's. I tried to look away, but I could even *hear* the couple as they ate. I imagined the smacks, the groaning, the sighs and heavy breaths taken between oversized bites. I alerted Billy and together we counted. 1...2...3...4,5...6,7...8 Big-Mac wrappers total.

We stared in amazement; our mouths wide open. Billy turned to me, for only a moment, letting go of my arm.

"I am totally imagining them having sex right now," Billy

laughed, "Eww, Etch-a-Sketch," he said, shaking his head back and forth rapidly, trying to rattle the image from his mind.

I was also imagining them having sex, and it was too much. I started to slip backward, my knees buckling atop my four-inch party heels. Watching the couple eat was one thing, but imagining them suckling one another's greasy, postcoital fingertips was beyond.

"Ouuhouhhh," I let out an awkward cry, reaching for Billy as I fell.

"Oh no you don't," he said, catching me just in time.

I readjusted my purse and donut, and straightened my dress as he lifted me back into place. I shimmied and shook off the near fall, nodding my head in the direction of the dive bar. I checked to see that I hadn't scuffed my stilettos.

"Girl. Buy yourself some snow boots already," Billy said as we continued on, carefully, toward the bar.

4

Auriane Tries Mescaline

I have always loved Valentine's Day, mainly for the outfit options. You guys know I love to serve a *lewk*. On this particular Valentine's Day—I was sixteen—I wore my grey UFOs, a bright red tube top with three straps across the back and whatever matching tennis shoes I could best dance in. I had my hair in two, long blonde pigtails, and twisted up strands of hair, securing them with red heart-shaped stickers. I threw glitter all over my body, put on as many stackable candy bracelets as I could and boom. I was ready to go to the club.

At the time, my favorite spot was The Edge. Nation, the club across the street was more popular, but the Edge was way more fun. All the security guards were drug dealers, and didn't care that we were teenagers on Ecstasy. My girls and I basically ran that club, I'm not even kidding. It was me, my best friend Chelsea and our other best friend Frances. Chelsea is a hot brunette with huge boobs. I was an athletic blonde, and Frances is a smoking hot Asian girl. We were like a trifecta of sexual fantasy, and we were only sixteen. We preferred to think of ourselves as the Power Puff Girls, because yeah, we were *children*. Whatever the case, it worked in our favor and everyone respected us immensely. We got free drugs, and were treated like club kid royalty.

That night, I decided to take Mescaline. I had never tried

it before, but I really loved tripping, so I wasn't too concerned or cautious. I was in love with this guy, Paulie. He was, like, ten years older than me and he was into me too. Looking back, he's a gross loser. But I was into that back then, and besides, we'd only ever make-out, probably because his old ass knew that anything more would make him a child molester. Anyway, I reallllly liked this guy. He was cute even though he sorta' looked like a Keebler Elf. When he would take Ecstasy, he *really* looked like a Keebler Elf. Paulie's jaw protruded out so far, we used to joke that you knew when he was high because his chin walked into the room five minutes before he did.

Chelsea, Frances and I did the usual rounds at the Edge. We danced, a funny little hopping kind of dance that was popular in raver clubs at the time, showing off our wide leg pants and glittered torsos. We socialized, commenting on everyone else's outfits. People really outdid themselves. One of my close friends, Jacob, served a hilarious lewk that night; he wore an airbrushed t-shirt from Ocean City, and he had shredded the ends of the top and put pony beads on each shredded piece. It was amazingly bad. Jacob was always full of surprises. Once, when I was really high, tripping my face off, Jacob pulled balloons out of his pocket and one of those inflate-y things and made balloon animals. Talk about blowing my mind, right? But, that's a story for a different day (or page 102, actually). Back to Valentine's.

We danced around from room to room and caught up with all our people. The sun was coming up and we decided, since we were all still wide awake, to head back to Paulie's apartment for the after party. Once we got to Paulie's, it was time to take off some of my Valentine's Day costume and relax. I ate Ecstasy in conjunction with the Mescaline and I was feeling really good. I wanted a bubble bath but I also wanted to talk to everyone in the room about *everything ever*, so I stayed put. I was sitting with Paulie who was in sweats with no shirt on.

Frances was getting a backrub from Nate, a sorta' meathead guy who was in the same Fraternity with Paulie at the nearby University of Maryland. Chelsea was hanging out with Mike, who we nicknamed Junx, I didn't want to know why. Someone had put on Dave Ralph, probably one of the Transport albums. Melodic, slowly building Trance music filled the room.

I felt weighed down by the twenty or so candy bracelets I had on, and started to take them off. I removed each bracelet meticulously, holding it up and examining its sparkly beads. I then placed the bracelet in a pile with its friends on Paulie's chest while he reclined.

My eyes were huge. Like, totally blacked out huge. I was very happily cross faded on some good shit. After I removed all the bracelets and placed them on Paulie's chest, he was pretty much covered. To me, he looked like he was drowning in a sea of candy.

"Ahem," he said, looking at the pile on his chest.

"Oh, hunny! I'm so sorry! You're drowning!"

I started to pick up each bracelet one by one. I stopped again to admire each sparkly bead as I did. I eventually got them all off and put them on the floor. But when I turned back to kiss Paulie, I saw there was one pink bracelet left on his chest.

"Oopsie Daisy," I said in a sing song voice, and grabbed at it.

But it was stuck. I pulled harder, but it was really on there. I pushed my other hand against his chest and really gave it a hard tug, grunting, giving it my all, but this thing wouldn't come off! It was then that I realized Paulie was yelling. He was shrieking something fierce.

"What the fuck are you doing?" he asked me.

I shook my head and my wildly distorted vision cleared a little. I then saw, that wasn't a sparkly pink bracelet on Paulie's chest, after all. That was his nipple! Man, was I tripping.

5

Our Friend Jason: Part 1

"Ugh, I am just so sick of this whole hookup thing," I sipped on my mandarin Gimlet and stared up at the illuminated screen above the bar. Kelly Clarkson's 'Since you Been Gone' was blaring in another pop video montage.

"That's gonna' be a hit," I pointed.

"She seems sorta' basic to me," Jason replied, "Very Midwest. But you never know. Anything can happen."

A few pretty young things came and greeted Jason at the bar, both under 25 with deep chocolate skin and perfect six-pack abs. Both were in their underwear and topless.

"Boys, this is Auriane. Auriane this is..."

"I'm Terell," one man outstretched his hand and daintily shook mine.

"I'm Miss Jhene," the other introduced herself, her lip-gloss a glittery pink, and a small tiara perched on her head, "Oh wait, don't you work here?" She asked.

"Yep, just up here in the Video Bar mostly. Disco on Goth night," I answered.

"Ooh, there's so many straight boys on Goth night!" Miss Jhene beamed.

"Eh, straight-ish," I said.

"I know, right?" Jhene laughed, "Anyway,"

"We're doing the Wet Underwear Contest," the two said in unison.

"Be there, dahling," Miss Jhene leaned over and kissed Jason on the cheek and slid a small bag of cocaine into his hand, winking at me.

"We'll try to meet you. Right now, I'm giving Auriane love advice," Jason replied.

"Well, either way, so very nice to meet you," Terell kissed me on the cheek.

Jhene did a little curtsey. The two left Grand Central's Video Bar together and headed downstairs to the Disco.

"Those two are hot," I said, "Talk about body."

"They're great. And they have good coke. Double whammy," Jason looked up from inspecting the little plastic baggie, "Bathroom?"

"Eh, sure."

Grand Central had a total of four bars under one roof. There was the Pub, the Disco, the Leather Bar and the Video Bar. The Video Bar was the slowest bar in the complex with a locking, unisex bathroom. It was a great haven for all kinds of people to buy, sell and use drugs, as well as go to the bathroom (and exist) without having to gender-identify. Really, the Video Bar was ahead of its time.

As Jason hoovered down a few lines in the only bathroom stall, I washed my hands and lamented about my pathetic love life.

"There was the one guy who actually kept asking me out, but then I lose weight and he's gone. Like, totally gone," I stated loudly enough for Jason to hear over the thumping Circuit House.

"Ah, a Chubby Chaser. Well, NEXT," he replied.

"And there's plenty of guys at school, but all they want to do is hook up. Like come over, my Netflix came in the mail...And I'm clearly not gonna' find anyone working here."

"Right, like, hello, buy me dinner first. Also, no Goths. Sorry, but no," Jason said, punctuating his reply with a few sniffs.

Jason exited the stall.

"Did you do the whole bag?" I asked, impressed.

"It was short. Good, but short," he said, raising an eyebrow at me, and tossing the remnants of the bag my way, maybe two bumps.

"Look, Auriane. Guys are gonna' try to get sex as easily as possible. That's just nature," Jason started.

"I know that but—" I was fidgeting my car key into the baggie.

"Don't interrupt. Look at me. I have guys I treasure, guys I befriend and guys I call to simply fuck. And I didn't label these men. They labeled themselves by how they interact with me," Jason was meticulously washing his hands and checking his reflection in the mirror.

"Okay, yes, agreed," I finished the last of the cocaine and turned with Jason as he took my arm.

He pushed the bathroom door open, hard. The booming music flooded us. We stepped out into the bar, the cheap lights twinkling, the room more alive now than ten minutes ago. A few trans women sat quietly sipping their drinks at the bar as Kylie Minogue danced in an all-white hooded outfit on the screens above.

"I just had a fabulous idea," Jason said excitedly.

"Kylie Minogue dance party?" I asked.

"No," Jason rolled his eyes.

"Wet underwear contest?" I assumed.

"No. I mean yes, of course, but no. Let me take you on a date!"

"Ha, sure, yeah like we always do?"

"No, a real date. Let me show you how it should be done. The people getting dates, it's because they expect a date. They would never settle for less, and it shows. Let me take you on a date so you have a marker for what is to be expected. Like a blueprint for men to follow. Straight guys are into things like blueprints, right? Trust me, it'll be fabulous!" Jason gushed.

"I'm in no position to turn down a free dinner," I replied.

"Yes! And we'll go somewhere healthy so that tragic Chubby Chaser doesn't try and come back," Jason smoothed his well-manicured chinstrap goatee, "Now... Disco?"

"Disco."

Jason and I watched as a handful of beautiful young gays competed in the Grand Central Station Wet Underwear contest. Each contestant stood, in a pair of tighty-whities in a kiddie pool on the Disco stage. The host, a cute blonde friend of ours named Greg, would announce each contestant, and then gently pour warm water into their underpants. The contestant would do a little dance, and show off their...well, their dicks, mostly.

Jason and I cheered loudly for Terell and Miss Jhene, but

as usual the twinkiest white boy won the contest again. I called it a night, and left Jason and Terell to walk a few blocks home to my Mount Vernon apartment on Cathedral Street.

As I walked, I clutched my keys in my fist for an air of protection, nodding and smiling to the Trans prostitutes perched on each block. There were two groups in my neighborhood, the Pink Stars and the Blue Stars. They were rival gangs, but both sides frequented Grand Central, especially the Video Bar. We were friends in that bartender/patron/don't be a NARC kind of way, and they were protective of me when I walked home. I appreciated them immensely.

Baltimore is dangerous. It's good to have friends.

***

Our date was exceptional.

Jason picked me up at dusk, and rang my buzzer. He waited patiently for me to wing my eyeliner and come down a few minutes late. He stood with a beautiful bouquet of pink and white Peonies in his arms, dressed in an ecru linen suit perfect for the humid, August night.

"Oh, should I run back up and put these in water?"

"Don't bother. We can make a big deal about putting them in water at the restaurant and show off a little," he told me, putting his arm in mine.

We walked a block to his car, a Lexus that he had cleaned for the occasion. He opened my door, and put on downtempo Chicago House music at a low level.

"Ready?" He asked.

"Ready," I smiled, holding the pretty flowers in my lap.

We arrived at Helen's Garden—a quaint but Zagat reviewed boutique restaurant in Canton Square. Canton Square was mostly restaurants, bars and boutiques surrounded by charming red-brick row homes. It was a more expensive part of the city, and predominantly straight.

"This is the kind of place I would expect a straight guy to take me," Jason said, gesturing for me to have a seat at our private patio table, "We'll start with the bottle of Chardonnay, please," Jason smiled at our waiter, "Oh, excuse me," he added, "I'm sorry, but we need a carafe of plain water as well."

"Yes of course," the waiter turned to leave.

"No, I'm sorry, not for drinking," The waiter looked puzzled, "The lady needs something to keep her flowers fresh, please. So maybe two carafes. Thank you so much," Jason was being genuine, he didn't sound like a dick at all.

"This place is adorable," I told him, leaning over the table.

"And it's delicious. Do you have any preferences or restrictions? I've been here a handful of times and if you'll let me, I'd love to order for you."

"I trust you," I beamed, looking around at the lush flowers and vines decorating the patio.

Jason ordered a grilled Caesar salad and too many small plates to count or recall. We feasted on tapas and finished two bottles of great Chardonnay. Jason asked me typical first date questions. He wanted to know where I was from, what I was in school for, even though he knew all of this already.

"It's practice. A good guy should ask you these things. If he doesn't show interest, walk out," he advised.

"Dessert?" Our waiter asked.

"We couldn't possibly," I told him.

"No, we will. The raspberry crème brulee, please," Jason added, "Even if we only take one bite, it's too good to miss."

We wrapped up dinner and went back to Mt. Vernon. Jason walked me to my door, and gave me a kiss on the cheek. I clutched the carafe of flowers to my chest. Jason had tipped extra to keep it.

"Alright, no more bad dates, right?" he said as I opened the heavy, antique front door to my building.

***

The next morning, I woke up early. I made coffee, and after opening the windows and scrubbing a few dishes left in the sink, I checked my phone. I had two texts.

One, was from Eddie. Eddie was older than me. We had started hooking up when I was 16, nothing very serious, just playful make-outs. I was now 21, and we had slept together a handful of times. Eddie was a photographer, which made him seem romantic but actually he was just emotionally unavailable. I read the text.

"want to see u."

The other text was from Jeremy. Jeremy and I were more involved, but he was unreliable. He had a way of showing up just when I had grown tired of him not showing up; that manipulative sixth-sense that tingled when a girl was ready to move on. He was mysterious, troubled and sexy. He was also not very nice to me. I read the text.

"What are you doing for your birthday?"

Eddie's text was clearly a booty-call, but Jeremy might actually want to do something for my upcoming birthday. I thought about responding, the text cursor blinking at me like a countdown.

"I'm not sure yet...what do you have in mind?" I waited.

"We should chill."

I looked around the room. I looked at the photos of friends on the fridge, and the pretty paintings set above the antique cabinets in the kitchen. I thought about a response. I then looked over to the kitchen table. There were Jason's Peonies. I tossed the cell phone in my purse—text messages unanswered—and got ready for class.

"No more bad dates..." I said out loud.

6

Our Friend Jason: Part 2

"What the fuck are you doing?!" I yelled, watching Jesse empty my suitcase out of his second story window, my summer dresses floating down onto Charles Street.

"Are you goddamn actually crazy? What the fuck!" I threw my hands in the air.

"Crazy, yeah I'm the crazy one," he spat back, "Who comes all the way here just to say you don't want to be here? You can get the fuck out!" He yelled.

"Fine! Fucking fine you insane person!" I said, grabbing my keys from the kitchen counter and slamming the door behind me.

I raced down the stairs, hoping to rescue some of my dresses from the traffic below. Charles Street was busy and I was sure my outfits were being destroyed. I was in a panic. Cars were smashing some of my favorite all time lewks. A few of my items had drifted into trees and planters lining the streets. I ran over and started to stack them over my forearm.

"Probably fucking covered in dog piss," I muttered to myself as people walking by gawked.

There was a red light at the intersection and I took advantage of the pause in traffic to run and grab a few pieces of my wardrobe. The light changed and people honked rudely for me to get out of the way. I started to cry.

"Oh my God," I heard from a nearby car, "Auriane de Rudder what in the Hell are you doing out here?"

I looked up to see my old friend Jason. He put on his hazard lights, and got out of the car, ignoring people honking behind him.

"No, no, no. What is this? What is all this?" he asked, pawing at the ruined clothes I held, "And are you crying? I thought you moved to Chicago? What is going on?"

I burst into tears, harder this time. Just as I did, Jesse threw my purse from the window.

"Fuck you!" he yelled as the bag landed on the sidewalk and burst open, my wallet, money and tampons strewn for everyone to see, "I hope I never see you again!"

Jason hurried over to the bag, and quickly shoved everything inside.

"Get in the car, right now," he ordered, "Fuck you, asshole! Do you know how expensive her dresses are? Fuck you!" Jason yelled up at Jesse's window, now shut.

Jason drove us in silence for probably 15 seconds. It seemed longer. I just stared out at the city streets, watching as we drove from Mount Vernon into Charles Village.

"I have some errands to run, but clearly you can't go back to whatever that was," he said gently, turning off of Charles Street and pulling up to pretty row home, "Stay here, I'll be right back, okay?"

"Okay," I sniffled.

Jason popped open the glovebox and pulled out a pack of tissues, "Here," he said, placing them in my lap, "Don't worry.

We can hang out all day. When I'm done with my errands we can brunch or something."

Jason walked from the car and into the home. I stopped crying to assess what I had saved from Jesse's freak-out. All of the clothes were ruined—to some degree—either by tears or tire marks or general street grime. My wallet was intact, and I had my keys—both a set to my apartment in Chicago and a set to Jesse's apartment in Baltimore. I did not have my cell phone. When I realized this, I started to cry again. Jason stepped out of the rowhome, tucking something in his inside jacket pocket. When he saw I was crying, he walked faster, and broke into a jog toward the car. He opened the door, and sat down and exhaled.

"So, should I even ask what happened?" He asked.

"He...he has my phone. I can't call anyone. I don't even know who to call. He was supposed to drive me to the airport tonight."

"What kind of phone?" Jason asked.

"It's just a Nokia. It's cheap."

"Okay so you can just get another one. We're not going back there, right?"

"Right," I nodded, wiping away my tears in his passenger side mirror.

"I can drive you to the airport. What time is your flight?"

"Not until 8:30," I said.

"Fabulous. We have all day together," Jason smiled, "Okay I have two more stops and then I'm all yours."

We drove through the city, making two stops- one in a sketchy part of the West side and another on North Avenue near the Station North Arts building. Jason also made a quick stop at his apartment in Bolton Hill. I stayed in the car the entire time, slowly regaining my composure, grateful that Jason had appeared when he did.

"Okay. Errands are done. I was supposed to meet my mother for brunch, but I can reschedule if you're not feeling up to meeting her right now."

I had never met Jason's mother, but I knew they were very close. He always spoke of her glamour and poise and her fantastic head of thick, blonde hair. I had seen a picture once on Jason's fridge. Daria had perfectly manicured French tips, wore a huge diamond ring and had a bright, white smile. I was dying to meet her.

"I'm in. Do you think I look okay?"

Jason looked me over. I had no makeup on and my hair was in a sloppy bun. I was wearing a loose boatneck t-shirt and leggings. The argument between Jesse and I had happened well before my 10 a.m. shower. I watched Jason assess me. I pulled out a single tube of red lipstick from my purse. I put it on and shrugged.

"Perfect," he said, and meant it.

***

Jason passed away from a stroke on February 11th, 2020. We hadn't seen each other in years. The news sent everyone who loved him into a spiral of shock and sadness. We all imagined, no matter how long it had been, that we would share a cocktail and a charming evening with Jason again. While I know I can't do that now, I have faith that it'll happen someday, in the unknown. And I *know* that Jason will recommend the very best martini bar as soon as I get there.

7

"Please, Take me to the Mall…"

I tell this story in person a lot, because it's short and I can spit it out between drink orders at the bar. Also, my old-man regulars love to find out that I applied to be a stripper, although they're always disappointed to hear it didn't work out. Anyway, so here's a quickie about the time I tried to become an exotic dancer. Also, an aside: Forgive any typos today. I have super long, glittery nails because it felt right for writing about stripping, amirite?

I was living in Chicago and I was not having a great time. I had been fired from my first awful, corporate job. Then, when 2008 hit and the economy ate shit, I was laid off from my subsequent start-up job. I was living alone--broke and lost--in a freezing cold city I couldn't stand.

My neighbor Maya, who was beautiful, confident and happy stopped by one day to check on me as I wallowed in my unemployment. Maya had just gotten a breast augmentation and was off work for a week. Maya was a stripper.

We lamented over lost money; mine my paycheck, hers, her tips. Talking cash reminded me of a time before my corporate life. It was a better time, a reliable time when I worked for tips instead of the wildly unpredictable world of paychecks during a recession. It was funny. People were always asking me, when I was a bartender, when I would 'get a real job.' I had now had two, and they left me more unstable than bartending for cash ever had.

"I'll just go back to bartending," I told Maya, "At least it's reliable."

"Or you could always strip," she said, kissing me on the forehead as she picked up her thick, faux fur coat from the sofa.

"Yeah right," I replied.

"Seriously, let me know, I'll vouch for you," She opened the door, letting a gust of icy air in.

I hunkered down under my blankets on the couch. I had never really thought about stripping, before.[1] But now? Why not? It's not like I knew anyone in Chicago, really. No old acquaintance was going to saunter into a club where I was shaking my ass. All the people I *had* met in Chicago were of little significance. I had one or two friends who wouldn't judge me, and a bunch of random people whose opinions meant nothing. If my old bosses showed up, it would be funny. Like, 'You laid me off and now look what I have to do...' I already hated my dad(s), so I had the proverbial Daddy Issues needed to work a pole. What did I have holding me back? My significant other didn't treat me very significantly, so fuck him. Even if it went horribly wrong, I'd have something new to write about.

So, I did it. Or at least I tried.

1. ^ *Professionally, anyway. We all know what happened in Nogales*

I went to VIPs in Lincoln Park on Thursday afternoon. I met with a manager there, Tony, who told me to come back in on Monday night to audition.

"Look, the try-out is straight forwahd. Ya' show up and ya' strip. Don't chicken out or throw up, and remembah to take ya' clothes off. Bam, ya' hired," he told me, "Just ask for Big Tony when ya' get here, any time aftah eight."

At home, I tried on all my sexy underwear and finally decided on an all-black lingerie set with little bows and garters that I let hang loose, unattached. No one at the office wore pantyhose anymore, and I figured it was the same at the strip club. I practiced a few moves in my highest heels in the mirror and mentally prepared myself. I didn't tell Maya, in case I caved. She was so magnetic, and I didn't want to embarrass myself in front of someone I admired so much.

Monday night arrived. My friend Garin agreed to accompany me to the club. Garin is one of the friends in Chicago who *did* matter, one of the non-judgey ones. We arrived around 10 pm. I brought a copy of my resume, because that's what I always did when I wanted a job. It's professional.

Tonight, Tony was distracted. The club was busy for a Monday. He took my resume, and looked it up and down.

"I'm here to audition," I told him.

He looked at me. He looked at my resume. He looked at me again.

"Have a seat," he said shaking his head, again looking at my resume.

My resume did not have any strip clubs on it. It had HR work for a major corporation and a small software company listed under a bevy of computer skills and other attributes I thought were universally appealing. Who wouldn't want a stripper who was timely, came highly recommended *and* knew how to program? Hello? It's called *layers.*

Garin and I sat. We sat for a long time. The club got less busy. Tony walked by several times. He didn't make eye contact with me once. After a few cocktails (2 drink minimum, guys) I left Garin at the table and approached Big Tony.

"So, should I audition now?" I asked him, my duffel bag full of panties and heels hanging off my shoulder.

"Kid..." he paused and took a breath, "You brought a freakin' resume," he looked me in the eyes, "Get outta' here, why dontcha'?"

I was mortified. Possibly more mortified than if I *had* stripped. Who did this guy think he was? I was a *woman*, a full-grown *woman*. I brought a thong *and* platforms. I practiced my sexy dance, for Chrissakes. And my resume was extremely well put-together, thank you very much!

I returned to our table defeated and told Garin we could go. We entered the foyer of the club, and as we pulled the thick, velvet curtain closed behind us, a short man with dark features ran up to me. His black eyes looked wild, desperate. Beads of sweat were dripping from his furrowed brow. He then asked me, in a thick Middle eastern accent,

"Please, can you take me to the mall?"

Huh?

"What mall?" It's, like, midnight," I replied, thrown off by such a random request.

"Please! Take me to the mall!" He repeated.

"Dude, *what* mall? You mean the Magnificent Mile?"

"Please, I'll pay you! Just take me to the mall!" He was very animated now.

I guessed he really needed to do some shopping.

"Man, I don't know where you're gonna' find a mall. There's a CB2 over there," I pointed.

"I'll give you 100 dollars. Just take me to the mall!" He said, his final offer.

"Jesus, WHAT MALL?" I yelled into his sweaty face, "Ugh, never mind, no, we aren't gonna' take you to the mall, excuse us," I said, pushing past him.

I was over it. The whole scene.

"Fine," he said, "Bitches," he hissed and walked past the velvet curtain, into the club.

Garin and I walked toward the exit. As we passed the cashier in the front lobby—a pretty young woman in a corset who had witnessed it all—she called out.

"He shoulda' asked me," she said getting our attention, "For a hundred bucks? I woulda' kicked him in the balls."

Garin and I looked at each other in a fleeting moment of naiveite, our mouths open in little O's of understanding and shock.

"Oh. So...he didn't want to go to the mall," I said as we pushed out of the club, and back into the icy, night air.

8

Getting to Know Your One Night Stand: DON'T DO IT!

Warning: This is not literary. This is just the story of the worst date I have ever been on in my entire life. It was so bad it *must* be told. But, also, I don't ever want to have to speak of it again. So here ya' go.

I met the guy at Clancy's. Of *course* I did. I would meet the worst guy at the worst dive bar, right? I was working on a Saturday night, stuck behind the ring-shaped bar waiting on toothless men, some of them elderly, some of them not. My boss sat amongst them, rubbing his bald head, probably on speed, sucking on his teeth and watching me. A few young people were shooting pool, enjoying the lack of ambiance such a dive bar offers. Other than that, I was surrounded by hard alcoholics; people who had really given up, people with something to drink about. It was like if Dante's Inferno had a cocktail lounge. Then, in walked this cute guy.

Reynaldo was tall, dark and handsome, especially compared to everyone else in the room. He ponied up at the bar by himself and ordered something respectable—a beer and a shot, and not a Lemon Drop, either. I could tell he liked me. He leaned in when he talked to me, and I did the same, desperate to talk to anyone other than Bill, one of my needier regulars. Bill's breath smelled like something had died in his mouth. It *permeated*.

"So, like, what are *you* doing in *here*?" I asked him.

"Oh, I'm sorry, should I leave?" He smiled and pushed his shot glass toward me.

"Another?" I was already pouring the bourbon into the glass.

"Yeah, I can't stay long though. I'm here to meet a friend, then I'm not sure where we're going," he took a sip of the shot, "Cheers," he said.

I picked up a shaker full of vodka I kept hidden in the ice bin and poured myself one. I glanced over to my boss, who was now voice texting into his phone with a furrowed brow. I sucked down the shot while he wasn't looking.

"You just keep that there?" Reynaldo laughed and gestured at the shaker.

"Dude, look around you," I eyed three middle-aged men huddled together at the bar, dead drunk. One picked his nose, "You're Goddamn right I do."

"Cheers to that," he said and laughed and finished off his shot, "So, like, what's a girl like *you* doing in a place like this?" He asked.

I was smitten. What an apropos question. I mean, what *was* I doing in that dump? I tried to come up with an answer, something witty instead of depressing, but before I had to, Reynaldo's friend showed up. He was a she, and she was really pretty.

"Heyyyy," Reynaldo stood as the petite, brunette leaned into him for a hug.

"I'm sorry I'm late, it's one of those days, you know? I am, like, fifteen minutes behind on everything. I mean every single thing, I swear," she gushed, winded, as she took off her coat.

"Whew, I need a drink," she looked up to me.

"Oh, uhh, Lisa, this is..." Reynaldo looked embarrassed that he hadn't asked my name.

"Auriane," I told her and reached out to shake her hand, "Whattaya drinkin' lady?" I asked.

"Hi, I'm Lisa, nice to meet you. I am gonna..." she turned to Reynaldo and saw the beer and empty shot glass.

"Shots? Are we having that kind of night?" She asked Reynaldo, "Alright, then. Something fruity. And a vodka soda," she said.

I mixed her a concoction of flavored vodka and juices and made one for myself. I poured Reynaldo another bourbon and raised my glass.

"Sante," I said, and quickly glanced at my boss, still rambling into his phone with his eyes closed.

I gulped in unison with the couple, and like a good bartender I backed off. I figured the two of them had at least a casual thing happening. Backing off at Clancy's, however, didn't mean much. Hunched over the adjacent sink and, scrubbing dishes, I couldn't help but eavesdrop. It's a small bar. Voices carry.

"Oh, yeah, things have been good, you know, everything with my dad finally settled down, and he's doing pretty good. So that's a huge relief," I heard Lisa say, "What about you? How are your sisters?"

As I scrubbed, the two mostly talked about family and mutual friends. I heard a grumbling from the other side of the Inferno and turned to see Bill, waving his empty Bud Light bottle at me. I grabbed another and brought it over to him.

"It's about Goddamn time," he said, and inhaled a sip, leaving a rim of foam in his white whiskers.

He let out a long, silent burp, and blew it at me.

"Jesus, Bill," I said, "That's why we all take our time bringing you another one."

"O!" He barked back.

That's what he called me. 'O.' He was never sober enough to learn my name.

"Yes?" I asked sweetly, sarcastically changing my tone, my hands on my hips.

"Urrrreeerruuupppp," he let out a long, loud burp.

"Keep it classy, B," I said.

I poured Bill and myself two more of my 'secret shots,' and toasted him. The clientele at Clancy's could be disgusting, but I knew how to make money.

I went back to the sink to wash dishes/eavesdrop on Reynaldo and Lisa. I tuned in and out as they filled the air between them with inane chit chat and then—

"I don't know why, but my poops really don't smell bad," Lisa said.

"Umm. Yeah. They do." Reynaldo and I simultaneously responded.

I looked up, embarrassed that I had chimed in, but I couldn't help it. This girl actually just said her shit doesn't stink! Come *on*. Reynaldo looked at me and smiled, thinking the same thing. In that awkward moment, whatever Lisa and Reynaldo had between them had been replaced.

"Do you just want to stay here?" Reynaldo asked his friend.

"I mean we can. Do you guys have food?" Lisa asked.

I smiled at Reynaldo. He smiled back and held my gaze. Neither of us even looked at Lisa.

"The burgers are good," I told her, still staring at Reynaldo as I handed her a menu.

"Are you working all night?" Reynaldo asked me.

"Yep, every Friday and Saturday night and then Sundays for football."

"Shit, all weekend?" Reynaldo made a sympathetic face.

"Oh, Hun, it's a good thing. Any bartender worth her salt wouldn't have it any other way. I'd say let's hang out on Monday but I'm—"

"I'm flying out on Monday," Reynaldo interrupted me and also took the words out of my mouth.

"Dude, that's what I was gonna' say. I'm flying out on Monday. I'm going to visit my friend, she just moved to Portland," I turned to Lisa, "Did you see anything you wanted to eat, Hun?"

"Girl, that's crazy," Lisa said excitedly, "He's flying to Portland on Monday, that's where he lives," she took a sip of her vodka soda, "Oh, and the ABC burger sounds good, medium well?"

"Are we on the same flight?" I asked Reynaldo as I nodded at Lisa's order.

We determined that, no, we weren't on the same flight, but

after a double jinx—the poop one, and the travel one—it was clear we would have to sleep together. I mean, we had *so* much in common.

Also, an aside—There is something I call the Slim Pickens Theory. The Slim Pickens Theory is the theory that, when you're in a room full of boogins, anyone mildly attractive looks fine as Hell. It's similar to being an LA 2 but an Oklahoma 10, you get it? Or, like, remember in high school, how all the girls thought Mr. Belardi was hot? But in reality Mr. Belardi was just an average math teacher who happened to be 20 years younger than the rest of the staff? Right. Slim Pickens. You are as hot as your surroundings. So, at Clancy's? Reynaldo was red hot, baby.

Despite the horniness in the air, Bill's breath was also still lingering and I had a job to do. I gave Reynaldo my number, and left him and Lisa in peace to eat their burgers. The night went on, and by closing time, I was pretty drunk on 'secret shots.' I wiped down the bar, turned out all the lights and locked the doors. I picked up my phone to call an Uber, but was interrupted by a text from Reynaldo.

"Hey. Are you done with work yet? I'm having drinks at the hotel if you want to come join," the text was accompanied by an address.

I'm really not down with OPP, meaning Other People's Places, so I declined. But, as they say, when one hotel door closes, an apartment window opens.

"I have champagne at my place," I texted back. I sent my address and finished ordering my Uber.

The sex was pretty excellent one night stand stuff. Reynaldo was cool, fun, a good kisser and had a big dick. He had zero aversion to using condoms, and used them correctly—which, as we know ladies, is terrifyingly uncommon. There was one kink—and I'm going to say this in Spanish in case my mom (or Reynaldo, but we'll get to that later) is reading this. Reynaldo was very into...mi culo.

Butts are in right now, and I have noticed that recently more and more guys are into culo. So that wasn't *so* shocking. But Reynaldo was more interested than most. Reynaldo needed to really look at it. Not just take a peek, give her a once-over. No. In order for Reynaldo to come, Reynaldo needed to stare deep into my culo.

Eh. Whatever. I let him.

The next afternoon, Reynaldo surprised me with a phone call. No one calls anymore.

"Hey, I know today is supposed to be awkward, but you seem really cool," he sounded rough and hungover.

"I am. Go on," I laughed.

"Well, do you wanna', like, keep in touch? I come back to Long Beach a lot and you said you travel to Portland."

"Sure man, I had fun last night. Good to meet a new friend, always," I told him and excused myself to get ready for work.

Months passed, maybe a year went by. Now and then, Reynaldo kept in touch through Facebook and would send me a funny meme or a nice message to say hello. Sometimes he was flirtatious but never overtly sexual. None of the memes were sexist or gross. I wasn't into him, but I wasn't into anyone else, so the casual flirting was welcomed. Plus, he seemed like a nice guy. A nice guy with a big dick who uses condoms and lives just close/far enough away? That's a good travel booty call.

One day, Reynaldo asked me out.

"Do you like Rufus du Sol?" he asked, "They're playing and I got tickets in November. If you wanna' come out to Portland, you can have one, be, like, my date. It's in three weeks."

I said yes. I have people in Portland, and why not? I wasn't seeing anyone special and I was bored with the monotony of my day to day.

I had also been trying to be more open when it came to men. I have a tendency to think they're all huge douchebags, and I was working on that. And yeah, Reynaldo would probably want to do butt stuff, which admittedly is not my thing. But he was a *nice* guy. Life is about compromise, right?

I stayed with friends for most of my trip, and planned to spend my last night at the concert with Reynaldo. He invited me to his place that morning and I followed up in the afternoon for details.

"What time should I head your way? Address? Or do you want to pick me up?" I texted him.

"UBER LIFE," he texted back.

What? I mean, I understand what an Uber is. And I get the message, take an Uber. But 'UBER LIFE?' Weird response, bro. Also, do I need to get the Uber? Is he sending an Uber? I mean, I'm not stingy but I did just fly to Portland. I felt like he could get my ride if he wasn't going to pick me up. I looked at my phone, he still hadn't sent me an address.

I looked over to my overnight bag, next to the front door.

Was I making a mistake? Should I leave my bag there, with friends, in case I needed an out? A reason to flee?

'No, no, no,' My inner optimist chimed in.

'You're learning to be more open. Not all guys are douchebags, Auriane. Give someone a chance. They might shock you. Just dive in. You are trusting. You are love,' she cooed.

"Address?" I texted back.

I plugged his address into the app and was surprised to find out that Reynaldo didn't live in Portland, but in a far, $50 Uber-away suburb called Beaverton. Ugh. 50 bucks? But I was committed to change.

'Hang in there. Believe. When something seems difficult, dare to do it anyway,' insert whatever mantra an idiot about to make a huge mistake may tell herself HERE.

'Besides, what's 50 bucks anyway? I mean, yeah, it's a night out drinking with friends in Portland, but you're going to have a great time with a nice guy. $50 is an investment in your future trust in men,' I listened to the idiot optimist in my head and ordered the ride.

UBER LIFE.

Beaverton isn't awesome. It's a standard suburb with ticky-tacky apartments and strip malls and trees and SUVs and chain restaurants. I didn't see any beavers at all. I arrived at Reynaldo's apartment and promptly had a panic attack—I get those—and tried to hide it with awkward conversation. Eventually it was all too much, and I turned to chugging two mango White Claws in rapid succession.

"We can walk to the bar down the street," he offered.

Clearly, I looked like an alcoholic.

"I can't drive. I got a DUI," he said.

This explained UBER LIFE.

Despite being outside in the fresh air, my panic held strong. As we walked to the local pub, I couldn't stop talking. I just went on and on and on. I'm always talkative, but this was rattled and bizarre. I knew I was being annoying but I couldn't stop. Note to reader: Don't mix panic and White Claw.

The bar was cute, and didn't look like a chain. We ordered vodka sodas (my liquid Xanax, thank Christ) and some appetizers. I kept on talk talk talking and an uninterested Reynaldo scrolled through his phone.

"I don't know why I even text this girl," Reynaldo cut off my rambling, still looking at his phone, "Maybe because she has sex with me," he added with a laugh.

'Wait. What?' My internal monologue piped in again, less optimistic now, *'Okay. Wait. Wait. What? I mean, I get it you are halfway through a panic attack and a sucky date so far, but you flew here for this. He needs to save his booty texts for tomorrow when you leave.'*

"I asked her to come tonight, but she isn't texting me back," Reynaldo put his phone down on the table.

'Huh? Oh goddammit, is this even a date? If it isn't that's fine but I thought he said date. Oh wait, are you expected to have a threesome tonight? A threesome and buttstuff?' I think my inner optimist turns pessimist when she drinks.

I felt my panic flooding back. The waitress brought my drink just in time.

"My coworker might come too, you'll like him," Reynaldo added.

"A foursome?!" I blurted out.

"What?"

"Nothing," I said and chugged half my drink.

I sighed and waved to the waitress for another vodka soda. I sipped the rest of my first in silence while my inner voice bitched me out.

'Why didn't you leave your bag at Shauna's house? What the hell were you thinking? Motivational mantras? What are you, on a corporate retreat? Trust someone? Open up? He's a butt guy, Auriane, he can't be trusted. More like open up your butt, you dumb bitch. Goddammit. Get your life together!'

"You are an asshole," I whispered to myself and sucked down the last of my drink as another arrived.

"Huh?" Reynaldo looked up from his phone.

"Oh. Nothing," I said softly.

We sat in silence for a few minutes, Reynaldo still immersed in his phone. I chomped on potato skins and calamari, trying to prevent the dreaded forgot-to-eat blackout.

And then, out of nowhere...

"Do you ever feel scared, like, it's all so fragile, like you might just snap one day?" He asked me, for once making eye contact.

What a terrifying question. I can deal with a little crazy, I get panic attacks, I get it. But was I sitting with a serial killer?

"No, not really," I replied cautiously.

"I dunno'," he took a sip of his drink and picked up a

potato skin, "Most days I'm fine, but there's little things that edge in, you know?"

"No. Like what? What edges in?" Despite being horrifying, this was the best/worst part of the date so far.

"Have you heard of Trypophobia?" he asked.

"I have not," I said, intrigued.

"It's, like, holes. Like, a lot of holes," he said and took a long pause to eat a potato skin.

I just sat there, waiting, wide-eyed.

"It makes me sick...Like the center of a sunflower or soap bubbles. It makes me wanna' fucking barf," he pushed away the small plate in front of him and took a sip of his drink.

"So, tightly packed holes? That's a trigger? For Try...po..." I was into this, this was weird.

"Trypophobia. Yeah. I dunno'. It's just crazy how easy it is to slip into madness, I guess..." he trailed off.

Reynaldo gestured to the waitress, "You ready to go?" he asked me, suddenly upbeat.

"One more, please," I asked the waitress awkwardly.

I took a moment to reflect. I was quiet, sipping my final cocktail, just looking at Reynaldo as he once again stared into his phone. My inner monologue was slower now, thanks to the vodka.

'So...the guy who is into staring into culos...is afraid of tightly packed holes?'

I laughed out loud, just a short little chortle.

'Trypophobia...slipping into madness...girl, you sure know how to pick 'em.'

"We better get going," Reynaldo signed the bill, "You got drinks tonight, right? I'll get this and the Uber there."

'I don't think this guy will kill you...I mean, it would make more sense to kill you in Long Beach, less clean-up for him. Plus, your last Uber went to his address. He'd get caught.'

"Uber Life," I replied and smiled.

At this point, I was fine with this being the worst, most expensive date ever. As long as no one 'slipped into madness,' and as long as I could safely get my suitcase later, I'd foot the liquor bill. So what if I flew here and Ubered to a suburb? Whatever. I was stuck.

'Just don't die. And make the best of it. That's what you do,' My inner optimist and pessimist had joined forces.

I could go into more detail here and explain that of course, the rest of the date was consistently not good. It did ebb and flow, getting better and then worse throughout the night, but it was all pretty standard crappy date stuff. This was also the LONGEST bad date of my life, so I'll summarize below. The good—err, really bad-- stuff comes after, I promise.

- We Ubered *back* to Portland. I know. UBER LIFE. Don't even get me started.
- Reynaldo's elderly, gay coworker joined us in Portland for the concert. He was a delight and a welcome distraction from Reynaldo.
- We hit a few bars.
- The concert was incredible. If you get a chance to see Rufus du Sol live, do it. They're gorgeous, sweet, talented, and they have great energy. So did the crowd.

Reynaldo refused to stand in the crowd and dance, and instead stood by the restrooms the whole time.

- We went to a sports bar afterward. The gay coworker--sort of my life raft--left. Reynaldo and I were both very drunk. We argued over whether or not to go to strip club. I was not in the mood to spend any more money. Especially not with this guy. (Also, we've had enough strip clubs in this book.)

- Back at the apartment we had one more argument, this one over what to watch on Netflix. I drank more mango White Claw.

- Finally, we went to bed. My bag was fine. No one got sick about holes, and no one was murdered. I'd live to see another day.

The next morning, I was up with the sun. I hopped out of bed, despite a pounding headache, ready to get anywhere but Beaverton. My flight wasn't for eight hours, but I was prepared to spend that time in the airport. I checked on Uber and was sad to see that the app was surging and would cost me $130 dollars.

"Do you want to get something to eat?" Reynaldo asked me, "You can drive my car."

I was hungover and anxious. I really didn't want to drive someone else's car, especially with them in it, especially especially if that someone was Reynaldo. My mind was too groggy to process.

"I know a great little Mexican place," he said.

"Whatever, sure."

Tacos did sound sorta' good.

We weaved through the uninspiring streets of Beaverton, Reynaldo giving me decent directions the whole way. He was less irritating today. He played good music in his car, and for a moment, I felt like maybe he wasn't so bad. Five minutes behind the wheel turned to ten. Then fifteen.

"How far is this Mexican place?" I asked.

"Actually," he said suddenly, "Pull over here," and he pointed, his first abrupt command on the ride so far.

I did as he directed and pulled into the lot of a carwash.

"I need a car wash," he said flatly.

I could not believe it. This motherfucker has me driving his car through a car wash? I just laughed and shrugged. I had given up.

"What's so funny?"

"Nothin' Miss Daisy," I said back as I struggled to pull the unfamiliar car into the automated wash properly.

"You need to back it up and ease back in," he told me, frustrated, just as I was doing exactly that.

"Haven't you ever been to a car wash before?" He rolled his eyes.

After the *fun* drive through car wash, we finally got some tacos. The 'great little Mexican place' was unremarkable. I ordered chicken tacos and water, and he got something more complicated. I sat at a dirty table with my tray of food, waiting with Reynaldo for his order to come up. I picked at some dried cheese stuck to the Formica table with my fork.

"Hey," he said, "I'm really sorry about last night."

I just kept picking at the cheese. I kept my head down. I didn't even want to look at this asshole.

"It's okay, I guess," I said.

"Diez y nueve?" A plump woman in an apron walked by us, holding a tray of food, "Diez y nueve?" She repeated.

"Is that your food?" I asked Reynaldo.

I picked up the receipt for his order and checked the order number. 19.

"I think that's your food," I told him as the woman passed by and called out again.

Reynaldo looked at me like I had thrown a glass of water in his face.

"Diez y nueve?" The woman called out, again.

"What? Are you fluent or something?" He asked in an accusatory tone.

Now hold on a second. This dude's name is Reynaldo Rodriguez, you guys. Just so you know. Okay? Okay. And I'm not judging because my name is Auriane de Rudder and I don't speak French, but...wait for it.

"I mean, yeah. I know enough to get by," I told him.

"Diez y nueve," The woman stood over us and looked at the receipt.

She picked up the receipt. She placed the tray of food on the table and shook her head at Reynaldo. She let out a sigh. Reynaldo narrowed his eyes and looked at me.

"I don't speak that Bingo Bango Jango," Reynaldo spat, and picked up his burrito.

Ya'll.

Bingo. Bango. Jango.

Okay, Reynaldo Rodriguez. Do you, Boo.

I wolfed down my taco and chugged my water. We didn't speak for the rest of the meal, or for most of the ride home.

"Do you need anything from the grocery store, Miss Daisy?" I asked as we passed an Albertson's near his apartment.

"Actually, yeah. Pull in there!" He wasn't kidding.

I laughed and shrugged. Why the hell not. Let's see what he's got left.

"I'm almost out of toilet paper."

This was actually the second time he had mentioned being out of toilet paper. I didn't think about it the first time—it was right when I arrived and I was having a panic attack—but now it seemed strange. Especially because, from what I had observed, he had a full roll of toilet paper in his bathroom. I had to say something.

"You have a whole roll in your bathroom."

Then, and I am not mincing words here, he looked me dead in the eyes and said, "We need more. In case you need to take a BIG SHIT."

I pulled into a parking spot and sat with that comment for a moment. We were silent. I inhaled and exhaled a deep sigh.

"Reynaldo?" I asked him calmly, "Exactly how much poop do you think is in me?"

Silence.

"I mean, that's a lot of toilet paper," I said.

More silence.

"I don't know," he turned away and crossed his arms like a child, pouting.

"Girls always use so much toilet paper. I just assume they take huge dumps," he said.

I sat with that comment for a moment, too.

"Maybe that's because we use toilet paper when we pee?" I said, lifting my voice an octave on the word 'pee,' gently, like a pre-school teacher.

"Oh. Whoa," Reynaldo turned to me, "I honestly never thought of that. That makes so much sense."

There was, of course, more badness from there, but fortunately not much. Uber stopped surging and I got my bargain $70 ride to the airport a few hours early. It was a long drive, and trust that I lamented every ounce of this story to that lucky driver. One last shout out to UBER LIFE.

When I got home, I changed my Facebook profile picture to a cluster of soap bubbles. I also posted a beautiful pic of a sunflower on my Instagram, just in case.

I never heard any of that Bingo Bango Jango from Reynaldo ever again.

9

Ghost Party

The Capitol Riverfront neighborhood in Washington DC—that's what they call it now—is "Modern, airy, and fresh," according to a cheery website on the subject. Buildings offer 360-degree views in a "perfect location." The neighborhood is touted as clean, safe and—my favorite term for not as ghetto anymore—*vibrant*. They have a Facebook. They have a Twitter. They have an Instagram. And yes, it's pictures of people doing outdoor yoga and cute dogs and then ice cream and red wine bars and then more dogs and then more yoga and more ice cream and even more dogs. It's downright curated. But there's something about the fastest growing neighborhood in South East DC that cheery website doesn't tell you.

The Capitol Riverfront is haunted.

***

"Lemon Wedge isn't gonna' call til' at least ten, probably later," I could hear the muted snap of Chelsea's gum against the back of her teeth as she awaited my reply.

"Okay, well I can come over whenever," I twirled the phone cord in between my fingers and leaned into the hallway, observing my step dad sipping on a Jack and Coke in his recliner.

"I highly doubt Larry's gonna' be paying any attention to where I go for more than another hour," I told her.

"Okay. Did you eat? I could eat. We could cook something," Chelsea chirped in her usual peppy tone.

"Yeah that works, do you have anything in the house?" I asked.

"Yeah some mac and cheese, maybe something for salad. Dina left some weird stuff from her latest diet kick. Ew, we have vegetarian hotdogs in the fridge and I swear to God I dropped one on the floor and it straight-up bounced. Like a pencil eraser."

"What the fuck? Oh, Lemon Wedge..." I laughed a little, "Maybe she'd grow some titties if she ate something...had a steak," I added, "From Lemon Wedge to Lemons."

Chelsea and I were best friends the way teenagers in movies are best friends. It was common that we would accidentally show up to school in the same outfit. We were often mistaken for one another by teachers and peers, despite looking nothing alike. We had best friend secrets, the kind we kept in pink, marbled composition books. We wrote in best friend code (Jack Cheese meant Jack Daniels, Blueberries was sex) and we hid things (liquor, drugs, love notes) in spots only the two of us knew about (under the hat of Chelsea's giant Paddington Bear doll, for one). More than anything, we were fiercely loyal to one another. We agreed to mutually despise anyone who threatened the well-being of the other; be it Homecoming queens, guidance counselors, bitter nerds, or, mostly, our parents. It was Chelsea and Auriane versus the world.

Getting ready at Chelsea's house was always more fun because it meant that her mother wasn't home. Dina would take long, mysterious trips with her boyfriends, sometimes leaving Chelsea alone for months. To be sure that Chelsea and I weren't getting into any trouble while she was away, Dina would call at all hours of the night to check in. To Dina, this was a clever tactic. If Chelsea and I were home and answered the phone at one or two a.m., clearly, we were in for the night, right? But parents are suckers and Dina—or Lemon Wedge, as we liked to call her on account of her tiny boobs--was no different. The parties Chelsea and I went to didn't get good til' at least three a.m., so Dina's tele-discipline didn't faze us.

Our outfits were very important. First, we had to have huge pants. Be they JNCO oversized pipe jeans or the thin, colorful parachute pants with reflective strips attached—UFOs--they were big and baggy and made for dancing. Chelsea and I matched our oversized pants with undersized crop-tops never larger than a handkerchief. We did all of this in candy shades of pink or baby blue or occasionally something metallic and space-y. This created a sexy but casual modern Lolita meets Judy Jetson thing. We were jailbait, but we were *really* cute.

Hair and makeup was also important. I'm tempted to put a picture here and save myself the proverbial thousand words, because we did some strange things to combine function with a *lewk,* honey. All you really need to know is this: The goal was to sparkle, but the goal was also to dance. For *hours.* Hair and makeup had to be shellacked by hairspray to stay put overnight. Yeah. We sprayed our faces with hairspray. Glitter was applied with the same and rhinestones, we glued individually to our faces using clear nail polish, although Superglue wasn't entirely out of the question. We braided our hair expertly, or pulled it up and back into pigtails so tight it made our eyes slanted. We then added glittering butterfly clips, baby barrettes, anything cute or sparkly that we could find.

If you haven't already put the baggy pants and glitter and the 3 a.m. thing together, in high school, Chelsea and I were Ravers.

The routine varied a little each week depending on which party or club we wanted to hit, but for the most part was consistent: Meet up, get ready, dodge parents, and go to the city.

"Hello?"

"Hi hunny, just checking in, what time is it there?" I could hear Dina's voice on the other end of the phone as Chelsea waved to alert me.

"It's almost midnight. We were just watching a movie," Chelsea leaned against her kitchen counter fully dressed, her hair pulled back in two tight braids and rhinestones glued in an arc across her forehead.

"Oh, you have company? What movie?" Dina asked.

"Just Auriane. Pretty Woman. Total classic," The key to lying to Lemon Wedge was to keep things simple.

"Alright honey, well I just wanted to say hi. It's so early here, only seven am, but I wanted to catch you before bed. Chelsea, the water here is so blue I can't believe my eyes. And the food! It's almost better than in Spain," Dina gushed as Chelsea rolled her eyes.

"Greece," she whispered to me, covering the end of the receiver, "That's great mom, I can't wait to see pictures."

"Okay honey, gotta' run, love ya' tons, byeeee," Dina squeaked.

"Bye mom, love you too," Chelsea said replacing the receiver, "Alright. Let's boogey," she said, her voice two octaves lower as she kicked off her slippers and slid into a pair of baby blue Pumas.

I didn't have my license yet, so Chelsea drove in her little red Honda hatchback. On this particular night, a Friday, we were headed to a huge, three-story warehouse in South East DC. On our way, we chain smoked and gabbed, listening to House and Trance mixtapes we had picked up at other parties. After about 45 minutes, we arrived in South East.

The streets were mostly abandoned warehouses, tow lots, dark alleys and rows of parked cars. Homeless people and crackheads lurked in between vehicles, peeking in windows and scattering if illuminated by passing headlights.

"Do you want to get out and get in line while I park?" Chelsea asked me as we cruised by our destination—the only lively building on the block, wrapped in a line of kids that looked just like us.

"Fat fucking chance," I laughed, "You're gonna' walk through South East by yourself?" I nudged her arm, "Yeah, I don't think so," I shook my head and lit a cigarette, watching as a nervous junkie ducked behind a car.

"Okay, yeah, duh, brain tumor. I don't know why I even said that," she shook her head as well.

"Ooh, a spot!" I pointed to a tow-away sign with a perfectly good parking spot below it.

"It's a tow away," Chelsea said.

"Yeah, but no one is gonna' tow until at least, like, 5 am, though, right?"

"You do have a point," she said, as she pulled into the spot.

"Biiiitch!" I heard a muffled voice coming from behind the vehicle.

I peeked in the side mirror and saw Ben. He was wearing an orange and green cropped baby tee and tiger-print faux fur pants. Around his neck was a black vinyl choker with a tiny diary lock in the center. He had painted gold glitter highlights on his cheekbones, and sparkled under the streetlamps. He looked adorable.

"Pop the trunk, it's Ben," I told Chelsea, hurrying to crank down my window.

"Hey babe, grab some of the 40s and help us, yeah?" I shouted to Ben.

Ben knew the drill, and while Chelsea and I did a final mirror check and junkie-proofed the car by hiding anything valuable, he unloaded a heavy cardboard box from the trunk.

"Hurry up, it's fucking cold out here!" Ben called out.

Before Chelsea and I had even locked the doors, the local bums had started to approach our car.

"Hey man," one man started with Ben, "Help a brother get a rock?" he asked.

"At least he's honest," Chelsea nodded to Ben, joining him at the cars open hatchback.

Ben handed the man a bottle from the box, "We don't have any Crack but we've got beer," he smiled gently.

"Just don't let anyone break into our car, okay?" Chelsea asked, raising her voice sweetly.

This activity--passing out 40 oz bottles of Steel Reserve to the bums of South East--was a weekly ritual for us. Each approaching bum was given a bottle, and each bum agreed to protect our car in exchange for the offering. We considered it making peace with South East. Most of the time, it worked.

When the 40s ran out, Ben, Chelsea and I scurried toward Nation, a non-descript, black warehouse building-come-nightclub with its name painted in stark white on its eastern wall. The club had different events on different nights of the week, and while a lot of people mistakenly called it "Nations," everyone in this Friday night line called it Buzz. The line was now even longer.

"Fuck," Chelsea said, walking toward the back of the line, "Where's Ricky?" she asked Ben.

"He's still parking. I saw you two and ditched him. He had a guy with him when he picked me up, they said they're going to Tracks first," Ben replied, talking through an unlit Newport 100 hanging from the side of his mouth.

"Why would anyone go to Tracks on a Friday?" I asked, reaching over to light Ben's cigarette.

"Whatever, anyway, there's something I didn't tell you," I said, "But it's not gonna' be a big deal," I turned to Chelsea, "I don't have an ID tonight."

"What? Why? What happened to your ID?" Chelsea held her arms tightly across her chest, shivering.

"Some bitch from Have a Nice Day Cafe took my backup last week. And my sister won't let me use her passport anymore. She's, being, like, *very* uncool," I said, pulling out a Newport of my own and lighting it.

"Too bad so sad," Ben taunted me, "What are you gonna' do?"

"I'll just do a passback, but I need to find someone who's at least blonde," I said scanning the line, "Ah, right there," I said pointing to a girl near the entrance.

I began pushing my way forward through the line, toward a girl who vaguely resembled me.

"Excuse me, sorry," I pointed toward the girl, "That's my sister, thanks, 'scuse me...sorry," I said, inching past my mostly wide-eyed, unfazed peers.

"Hey," I said and placed a friendly hand on the girl's shoulder.

"Heywhat'sup," she said at rapid speed as she turned around too quickly.

She was wearing a bright blue baby tee with the word SUGAR in iridescent bubble letters across her chest. She had on darkwash JNCOs and Adidas Shell Toes. Although she was significantly shorter than I was, we had the same long blonde hair, the same hazel brown eyes, and big, twin white smiles.

"I'mErica.Whoareyou?" She leaned into one hip, playfully holding a glistening grape Blow Pop in one hand.

"Hi, I am so sorry to bug you but I need the biggest favor ever," I said.

"Isaidwhat'syourname," she smiled and put the purple

Blow Pop in her mouth, rolling it against the back of her teeth.

"Oh duh, sorry. I'm Auriane."

"I'mgonna'callyouO," she said and linked her arm in mine, "Sowhatareyou,like,buttinginlineorsomething?"

"My name actually starts with an A—"

"Whatever.I'mcallingyouO.So,O,whatdoyouneed?"

"I need a passback. I can pay you 20 bucks if you want, or I'll get you a pill once I'm inside, totally your choice."

"Apassback,huh?LikemyID,right?Yeahokay," she said nonchalantly and pulled me closer, "You'llbe,like,mylittlesistertonight," she said and winked, "Paulie!Comemeetmynewlittlesister!" She yelled toward the very front of the line.

"Erica, can I bring my best friends up here?" I turned around and made eye contact with Chelsea and waved my hands for her and Ben to join me.

"Yeahwhatever,doyourthing.Paulie!" Erica called out again to a cute dark-haired guy as Chelsea and Ben snuck into the line next to me.

"Matt is back there but he's trying to find a passback, too. I told him to meet us later in the ladies' room," Chelsea informed me.

"Paulie,thisisO.O,thisisPaulie," Erica pushed her friend toward me, ignoring Ben and Chelsea entirely.

Paulie reached over without a word and gave me a huge bear hug, lingering a little too long, exhaling a trembling breath into my ear. It wasn't at all aggressive, just unexpected.

I looked to Erica for assistance and gently patted him on the back.

"Ohmygodpawsoff,Paulie,*sheeeesus*," Erica rolled her eyes and pulled on his shoulders until he unclenched me.

"Sorry," he said, his jaw askew and his green eyes wild, obviously from Ecstasy, "I'm Paulie," he shivered, his chin shaking as he spoke.

"He'salwayslikethiswhenherolls,like,so,sofuckedup," she said playfully as she mimed pushing his protruding jaw back into place.

We got to the front of the line and Erica performed a seamless passback, slipping me her ID in one hand while a meathead door guy tied a wrist band on her opposite arm.

Paulie and Ben went next, then Chelsea, then me. We knew it was safest to have a buffer between me and Erica since we were using the same license. Door guys aren't usually rocket scientists but also, it was a huge party foul to get a stranger's ID taken away.

Once we were inside, I slipped Erica's ID back to her.

"Thank you so, so much. Do you want the 20 or should I get you a pill?" I asked her as we entered the line for the security frisk, the second hurdle before entry into the club.

"Ohmygodshutup,it'sfine.BesidesPauliewillgetmewhateverIwant," she said, nodding toward him as he smiled a wasted, goofy grin.

I grimaced as a butch security guard ran her cold, gloved hands under my halter top and over my nipples. She smiled as she did it, revealing a bright gold front tooth.

"You're good," she said and patted me on the ass.

"Woo!Buymedinnerfirst,girl!" Erica laughed as she received the same treatment.

Chelsea kept her head down for the frisk, staring at the adjacent industrial trash barrel, filled with bags and bags of pills and powders. Ben was frisked in a separate line by male bouncers on the other side of the barrel. When a bouncer—male of female—found drugs, they tossed the bags into the huge, industrial can between them. It was almost full.

"OhJesusChrist,Igotta'go," Erica said pushing past us.

Chelsea and I laughed as she chased Paulie, who wandered alone into the crowded hallway. He floated, oblivious, his jaw shaking more now, that goofy grin on his face.

"Havefun,littlesister!" Erica called out.

"She's seems nice," Chelsea said, exiting the pat down and readjusting her bra.

"Right. Speedy. But nice," Ben chimed in, rejoining us.

Chelsea, Ben and I linked hands and walked through the cold hallway toward the red glow of the front room. The January air gave way to warm, humid fog-machine smoke and mixed with the aroma of a thousand sweaty dancers. The bass-heavy music got closer and louder and synced with a red laser light that hovered in the air. I watched as the light divided itself over and over again and swept through the crowd. We were in.

Our friends danced in unison, a sea of pulsating teens and twenty-somethings in baggy pants and visors. Light-up necklaces, hats, rings and glow sticks twinkled intermittently throughout the crowd. There was a lull in the music, an ambient mesh of peaceful sounds, and then a deep THUMP THUMP THUMP began.

"Oh my god!" Chelsea clawed into my arm a little with her nails, "Tai T!" She pulled me, hard, into the crowd and joined in the dancing.

"I fucking love this song!"

Chelsea hopped in time to the music, her braided pigtails bouncing, the glitter across her chest illuminated under the lasers. She waved to her favorite DJ, Tai, who nodded and smiled, crouched over his turntables. Ben was swaying just a little, getting used to the vibe of the front room. I scanned the dance floor looking for friends.

"I'll be right back," I shouted to Chelsea.

"What?!" There was another break in the music, the crowd slowed as blue and green lasers interlaced with the red.

"Abe is here. I'm gonna' go talk to him," I shouted to Ben.

"What?!" Ben shouted back.

"Do you want Acid?" I yelled to them both.

"Okay!" The beat dropped and Chelsea started to bounce again along with the rest of the crowd.

"What?" Ben asked again,

I rolled my eyes, "I'll be right back!"

"Okay!" Ben and Chelsea said in unison.

I walked toward Abe and made eye contact. I pulled my pack of cigarettes out of the cargo pocket of my hot pink UFOs, and held it up for him to see. I mouthed 'Join me?' and nodded at the patio door. Abe followed me outside, a few dancers in between us.

The patio was mostly deserted with the exception of two

girls smoking in a corner. They huddled together, shivering, their teen tummies and skinny arms exposed.

"What up girl how you been?" Abe asked as I lit a cigarette and leaned in for a reciprocal hug.

"Abe! Baby, baby, baby I've been good. Trying to stay out of trouble but not really, you know me," I exhaled a long stream of smoke and warm breath into the air.

"So, what's up, what do you want tonight?"

"Oh, alrighty then. No pleasantries," I nudged my friendly neighborhood drug dealer, "I see how it is."

"Nah, it's just fuckin' cold out here. You're all naked and shit, this shit don't bother you?"

"Ding!" I said and playfully flicked my nipples with my middle fingers. Abe and I both laughed, "Alright they're five tonight?" I asked.

"Yeah always, girl," Abe smiled and ran his fingers through the short locs that grazed his forehead.

I fidgeted with the Hello Kitty wallet in my pocket, "Let's do eight tonight," I said palming 40 dollars into his hand.

Abe returned the gesture. Standing close, he leaned down and passed eight paper hits of Acid into my pocket and gave me a quick kiss on the cheek. We didn't look like drug dealers. We looked like sweethearts.

"Hey Abe?" I asked.

"What's up?"

"How do you say your real name?"

"Oh my god, again? Auriane. Seriously? Of all the people who can't get my name right," Abe shook his head a little and laughed, his locs this time falling perfectly into place.

"Pleeeeeeeeease? I'm just always so fucked up when you tell me but I'm sober right now I swear to God. I'll, like, actually remember this time," I twirled one of my blonde pigtails around my finger.

Abe let out a sigh and crossed his arms.

"Ah. Ba. See. Abasi. It is *not* that hard."

I mouthed the syllables a few times and said it out loud.

"Ah. Ba. See. Abasi. Right?"

"Yes Auriane, you got it. Again," Abe leaned in and hugged me, "Go have fun, babe, lemme know if you need anything else."

I blew him a kiss and flicked my half-smoked cigarette on the ground.

Back inside I found Chelsea right where I had left her, the glitter on her torso now mixed with a thin sheen of sweat.

"What'd you get?" She shouted over the upbeat, Tribal House swaying her from side to side.

"Acid," I yelled back, "We need to go get Matt," I nodded toward the hallway leading to the ladies' room.

"I'm staying here for a minute. I'll meet you in the main room, yeah?" Ben shouted to us both.

Chelsea and I nodded and began dancing our way through the crowd, heading toward the main hallway. The club was a series of rooms connected by said hallway with the bathrooms right in the center of the action.

A typical night at Buzz was a bumblebee's flight from the front room—intimate, chill, small—to the main room—huge, packed, the main event. After we made our first trip from room to room, we went back and forth over and over all night. Of course, we stopped to do drugs in the bathroom whenever we passed it. Everyone did.

"Oh my God, finally! I've been waiting here to change my tampon foreverrrr. Where have you been?!" Matt asked us as he enthusiastically ushered us into the ladies' room.

He rushed to an available mirror and pulled out his keys and a small baggie. After fidgeting with the bag, he tilted his head back, and keyed a few bumps of white powder up his nose.

"Any $20 boogers?" He asked, turning to me and again tilting his head back.

"All clear," I said and rubbed his nose a little for good measure.

"Oh my God. So, it took me forever to find an ID tonight but luckily the girl I found was almost at the front of the line. Thank God because I was freezing my fucking balls off," Matt smeared iridescent gloss across his pouty lips, now talking to Chelsea and I in the mirror.

"Wait, a girl?" Chelsea asked.

"Yeah, scurrrrrrp, what did you say?" I added.

"Oh my God, yeah. She was so cute, a little lesbian girl. Very butch, but quite pretty," Matt's slight English accent came out on the words 'quite pretty.'

"You used a girls ID to get in here tonight? Absolutely no way," Chelsea laughed in disbelief.

"I was basically parading around yelling for literally 'ANYONE ASIAN' who would let me do a passback and she was, like, the only one. But it worked," Matt spun around from the mirror and faced us, "Gaysians have to stick together, girls."

"That is incredible," Chelsea said, lighting a cigarette and exhaling.

"Sooo, who wants Acid?" I asked Chelsea and Matt, but a few girls lingering in the bathroom perked their pigtails at my offer.

"Sorry honeys," I said in an affected, nasally voice and turned my back to them.

I passed two hits each to Chelsea and Matt and kept two for myself.

"Sante," Matt said, and did a spin, his silver parachute pants and fishnet top gleamed in the electric light.

"Cheers," Chelsea reciprocated as she and Matt placed the small tabs of paper on their tongues.

"Hey, speaking of Asians where's Frances tonight?" I asked.

"Frances said she's not coming out tonight. Something about her dad having another one of his Vietnam moments. I tried to convince her to come with us but she was tired from crying, I think," Chelsea said.

"Jesus," I said, and put the Acid on my tongue, too, "Why is her dad such a psycho?"

"Nay nay," Matt said, "Frances is at Tracks," he spun away from Chelsea and I and started toward the ladies' room exit.

"What? Why is she at Tracks? What's going on at Tracks?" Chelsea asked.

Tracks was across the street from Buzz. Occasionally they had good parties, but most of the time Tracks was either older and gay, for tweakers, or both. There was also The Edge which was across the street from Tracks, but the Edge wasn't for

Ravers on Fridays. I'm pretty sure they had actual pimp parties there on Fridays. You know, like, The Players Ball.

Matt pushed open the ladies' room door. Music flooded
in. The main hall was now packed with sweaty bodies.

"I don't know but I saw her and Angel when I was trying
to get an ID and they said the party's at Tracks tonight. I
know Ricky is there, too." Matt nodded his head to the music
as we navigated through the crowd and into the front room.

Chelsea blew quick kisses at passing friends as we made
our way. I stopped only when I saw Ben and our mutual
friend Melanie leaning on an empty dance podium next to the
bar.

"Hey ladiesssss!" I tried to make contact over the thumping bass, but it was too loud for anyone to hear me.

I pulled Chelsea, who in turn pulled Matt, over to our
friends.

"Found you!" I said leaning in to hug Ben.

"What's uppp!" Melanie erupted cheerfully, "What are we
wearing tonight?" she asked and did a playful pose.

A cute brunette pixie with a signature cropped hairstyle,
Melanie danced in front of us a little. She showed off her blue
vinyl halter top and khaki UFOs. Chelsea did a quick spin in
response, the silver ribbons on her baby blue pants momentarily in flight. She put her arms up in the air and showed off
what had to be 12 plastic candy-colored bracelets on each arm.
I mock-curtsied in my pink pants and white top. After our
mini-fashion show, we embraced in a three-way hug, covering
eachother's cheeks with glitter-lipgloss smooch marks.

"Are you sober?" Melanie asked as we were squished together by the swelling crowd of dancers, responding to the music.

"I'm tripping tonight," I replied.

"Me too," she said and grinned wider than usual, her pupils dilated.

The pulsing crowd pushed us further into the main room as the bass-heavy music and laser show continued to intensify. We stopped at a decent patch of available dance space and linked hands. We formed a small circle, carving out a space for our group.

The music ebbed and flowed. Trance anthems were broken up with more bass, more lasers and colored with ethereal intermissions. We hopped to the beat, doing our playful dance, twirling and kicking and throwing fists in the air. Each of us had a unique dance style, some of us had even practiced.

Melanie was getting good at Tutting, a walk-like-an-Egyptian inspired geometric feat involving a lot of arm stuff. Ben was more subtle, but I remember his turns were always my favorite—the way he would spin in his wide leg, fur pants, kind of on an axis, a little uneven and sweetly unrehearsed. Chelsea was curvaceous and sensual, but when she danced, she was childlike, playfully bouncing and making silly faces. Matt and I danced together, exaggerating and playing off each other. The room was wet with sweaty humidity and smelled like a musty basement.

"Do you want a bump?" Matt asked me, pausing from dancing and leaning toward me, revealing a tiny Ziplock baggie containing white powder.

"Coke?" I asked.

"K," he replied, now slightly hunched over, keying some of the powder up his nose.

"Nah, I'm good I'm just tripping tonight, I'm gonna' wait and see," I told him, "Actually, I'm gonna' smoke, I'll be right back. Chelsea," I leaned over to my best friend, and held up my pack of cigarettes, "Smoke?"

Chelsea nodded and we pushed through the crowd hand in hand, once again dancing our way toward the patio. We pushed through the double doors of the club and out into the winter night, steam rising off our bodies.

"Jacobbbbb!" Chelsea yelled out to another one of our friends, perched on a large planter, smoking in the center of the patio.

Jacob was dressed fabulously as usual, in light teal UFOs, and a white crop top. He had on a wash of light blue eyeshadow, and glitter under his eyes. His hair was gelled into glittery spikes lining his forehead. Chelsea dropped my hand and ran over to him, clobbering him with a giant hug. He responded by lifting her up and spinning her around and around until they both fell over into the planter, laughing. I lit two cigarettes and passed one to Chelsea.

"What's new, baby, how ya' been?" I asked Jacob as he readjusted himself on the edge of the planter, now with Chelsea sitting in his lap.

"Why are you smoking? You never smoke," Chelsea frowned.

"Ugh, I knowww," Jacob said, exhaling a plume of smoke, "I'm avoiding someone," he rolled his eyes, "Some trick."

"Uh oh. Boy trouble?" I asked.

"No, no, it's not like that. This guy…I've been staying with him and whatever he's alright, but he's, like, 40 and honestly," Jacob took another drag and crushed his cigarette into the planter, "He's just so annoying when he's rolling. I'm like, get offa' me, you know?"

"Ew, 40? Jesus that's, like, ancient…" My voice trailed off a little as I looked up at the sky.

The stars started to shine more brightly, vibrating in place, in sync with my heartbeat. I let out of a deep exhale. Deeper than usual. I watched my breath weave around the stars. Okay. I was tripping.

"Yeah dude, my dad's, like, 40," Chelsea added, taking a drag on her cigarette and also letting out an extra-long, deep exhale.

"Yeah, well it beats being at home and getting raged at and called a faggot all the time," Jacob stood up abruptly.

Jacob narrowed his eyes and cocked his head from side to side. He inspected us as he stood over us.

"Oh shit. Are you two tripping?" He asked.

Chelsea and I looked at each other and started to laugh, hard.

"My bad, oh my God! I'm talking about all this depressing shit! Oh, okay, okay," Jacob softened his posture, "Close your eyes, both of you," Jacob said and gently ran his hands over our faces.

Chelsea and I linked hands and did as instructed. We waited, eyes shut tight, listening to all the sounds around us—the chit chat of other Ravers, the bass of the music spilling out onto the patio, and now a strange, close squeaking, something foreign to the environment but also vaguely familiar. A moment passed and the squeaking stopped.

"Okay, open your eyes!" Jacob told us excitedly.

Chelsea and I were both expecting the same, tired party trick. Anytime you're tripping, some idiot comes up and waves a couple of glowsticks in your face to the beat of the music and thinks it's a life changing event. It's called a light-show and both Chelsea and I thought they were for amateurs. But Jacob wasn't an amateur. Jacob definitely wasn't an idiot. Jacob was Avant Garde. We opened our eyes.

Jacob stood there, proud and smiling a devilish smile. In his hands he held two balloon animals, dogs, and handed one to each of us.

"What the fuck?" Chelsea said before we both burst into unstoppable laughter, tears streaming from our cartoon eyes.

"Jacobbb," we heard a low, slurred voice grumbling somewhere on the patio.

"Oh fuck, there's Mr. Wonderful," Jacob said, caught.

Jacob unenthusiastically waved a fingers-only wave into the patio crowd. We watched in horror as a lumpy, dumpy old guy in khakis stumbled toward us.

"Oh no," Chelsea whispered, her mouth hanging open.

"I'll spare you an introduction," Jacob turned toward the wasted moans of his beckoning sugar daddy, "You girls have fun," he said.

Jacob mashed his teeth together into a wide, fake smile. He spun around dramatically and joined his date. I looked at Chelsea, visibly cringing, as the odd couple linked arms and walked away together.

"Let's dance?" I asked Chelsea, trying to shake off the moment.

"Yeah. Dance...Definitely." Chelsea said.

She pulled me into the pulsing patio crowd, and then another room and then another crowd, all of it blur and sweat and bass, until we found ourselves comfortable and safe, dancing with our balloon animals.

"Do you want some Coke?" Paulie, the cute dark-haired guy with the bad roll-face was now bobbing next to me, holding up a key and another small baggie of powder.

"Not really," I told him, smiling to show my appreciation, "I'm good, I'm tripping!" I yelled out as he danced closer and lowered his head to take a bump.

Paulie tossed his head back and inhaled. He stuffed the baggie and his keys back into his pocket. He looked up, wonk-eyed from drugs. He did his best to gaze into my eyes. He leaned in toward me, resting his arm on my shoulder and nuzzling my neck a little. We started making out.

Look. Making out or just being touched in general can go any which way when you're tripping. At first, kissing Paulie was going well. I was disoriented from the excitement and the vibe of the night. I enjoyed getting lost in the moment. It felt good to stand in one place and just *be* for a minute. But I was peaking. Tripping *hard*. The music started getting dark, transitioning from fun, danceable Breakbeats to creepy, monster-y Drum n Bass.

I pushed Paulie away and looked to Chelsea. She looked back, half entertained and half concerned. Paulie leaned in to kiss me again and I let him. What felt good at first quickly became annoying. As the music continued to change, things got creepy.

I looked at Paulie. His face in the laser lights was garish; that cocaine had not straightened him out at all. His pale, sweaty skin and shaky jaw were freaking me out. I reverted inwards, physically, recoiling as he clumsily pawed at me. I looked back to Chelsea. In contrast to Paulie, she looked angelic.

"Hey," I grabbed onto her shoulder like it was a life raft, "This is, like, the right Acid, but the wrong music, yeah?"

Paulies' hands were now gently wrapped around my waist from behind. To me, they felt like a waist chain you'd see on an inmate.

"Do you want to go to Tracks?" Chelsea asked me, her eyes like an actual Power Puff Girls'.

"Yeah," I pushed Paulie, who was now dripping off of me, away into the crowd. He barely noticed.

"Let's go get Frances," Chelsea took my hand.

Outside, the sky was a dark shade of blue instead of the wash of black it had been when we arrived. The sun would start to rise soon.

"Should we check the car?" I asked Chelsea as we walked.

"No, let's just go get Frances and then go," She replied, shivering as she walked a few steps ahead of me.

I took a deep breath in, and exhaled slowly, feeling the cold air rush out from my lungs. I watched it curl into steamy rainbows in front of me that dissipated as I walked through them. A crackhead darted behind a car.

"Where are we gonna' go?" I asked.

Chelsea stopped walking and turned toward me.

"We're going to Tracks," Chelsea said, very matter of fact, as if I was a dumbass.

"No, after Tracks. You said we'll get Frances and go," I stopped.

Chelsea turned around and looked at me, stunned and confused.

"Dude..." she said, exhaling her own plume of rainbow breath into the air, running her fingers through it, "I have no fucking clue," she said, leaning into me for a hug as she laughed.

We linked arms and walked together past the entrance to Tracks, through a sketchy alley and over to the club's fenced-in back patio. You see, if you waited long enough, there was no security on the back patio in the Winter, since the crowd had died down and it was too cold for most smokers. This meant that you could sneak in through a human-size hole someone had cut in the gate with wire shears. You just had to have someone help hold the gate to avoid getting scraped up. It wasn't comfortable, and you needed some luck on your side, but it was free. Chelsea's not-so-lucrative position working at the Columbia Mall Dippin' Dots afforded us only one cover charge per evening. The fence would have to do.

I tried to pull the fence outward, toward the alley to make room for Chelsea to crawl through, but it wouldn't budge in our direction. We needed help from someone on the inside. I scanned the nearly deserted patio. A tiny Asian girl with rhinestones lining her forehead was crouched in the corner, her arms crossed, smoking. She was looking intently at something--or maybe nothing-- on the cement below her. She looked up.

"Dude, fucking Eureka," I nodded toward the girl, looking at Chelsea.

"Frances!" Chelsea yelled.

The girl looked up and scanned the patio.

"Frances!" I repeated.

Frances looked at the stars above, as if the voice were coming from the sky. She then looked back down at the cement below her.

"Whoa..." she said, taking a few steps back, keeping her eye on the pavement.

"Fucking hello!" Chelsea chanted, "Earth to Frances!"

This time Frances looked in our direction. It took her a moment to recognize us through the fence but once she did, she snapped out of her haze.

"What up bitches?" Frances asked as she trotted over, dressed all in white.

"Hold the fence for us, we came to get you," Chelsea told her.

"Dude I thought the pavement was calling my name for a second," Frances dutifully held the fence, her eyes rolling back in her head a little.

"Dude, why are you here?" Chelsea asked.

"Everyone is at Buzz," I added as I squeezed through the fence.

"No, they're not," Frances said, "I just saw Jacob and some old guy, Angel is right inside and Ricky is here. Melanie is supposed to bring Ben and come meet him or so he says."

"Oh," Chelsea shrugged.

"Okay well lead the way, then, all knowing one," I did a Vanna White gesture toward the patio door and encouraged Frances to take us to our friends.

Tracks was slightly smaller, brighter and gayer than Nation. The music that night was more upbeat, less dark Drum n' Bass and more Deep House, Melodic Trance and, even in one small sub-section, some Happy Hardcore.

As we walked through each room, we saw our aforementioned friends. Jacob and the old guy were in the first room, gently swaying to a Mark Farina track. Angel—a petite, butch lesbian, dressed in an oversized polo shirt and muted cargo pants--was somehow dancing between rooms. I watched her spin back and forth. She ran her slight fingers along the brim of her white visor as she turned, one foot in the Trance room and the other at the precipice of the Happy Hardcore dance circle. I nodded to her as we passed by and she shined her signature crooked smile.

Ricky, our token hot-mess friend, was in the very back of the Deep House room. He had found a mirror and was transfixed, watching himself dip and spin as his arms and hands created an array of geometric shapes to the beat. I walked up behind him and watched. He dripped sweat, his jaw shaking, his skin pale. Yet, with every turn, he never lost eye contact with himself in the mirror. His dancing was impressive considering how extremely fucked up he was. I was just about to interrupt him, when I got pushed, hard. I turned to see what moron would dare to be so rude, but when I turned, I was pushed again. And then again. I was being flooded by people.

"Cops!" I heard someone yell in passing.

I looked for Chelsea and Frances but they were being pushed toward the exits, while I was being pushed toward Ricky and the mirror against the wall.

"Ricky!" I yelled, trying to break his trance, but he just danced on.

"Fucking RICKY!" I yelled again, closer this time, almost close enough to touch him. Harsh electric overhead lights flickered and snapped on, but Ricky just danced. Even the music stopped. I looked behind me and saw cops in their drab navy outfits pushing through the colorful crowd.

"Ricky!" I said again, grabbing his shoulders and trying to snap him into reality, "Ricky the cops are here."

He was still dancing, facing me and staring at me, now. His glazed sea-blue eyes were almost entirely black, his pupils the size of dimes.

"Auriane, just stop it," he said, high and clueless.

He turned around sharply and resumed his dancing, now to no music.

"Ricky we have to go, right now, I'm serious," I once again spun him around by his shoulders, desperate to talk some sense into him.

"Auriane...Puh..puh..puh..." He was stuttering badly.

Ricky let out a long sigh and spun, a choreographed turn and faced me. He stopped and scrunched up his face as if he was going to cry.

"Auriane. Puh...Pluh...please. Four...fou...Please just fo..fou...Please just four more minutes," he smiled a childish, closed-lip smile and tilted his head.

I couldn't help but laugh. Four more minutes? How very specific.

"Fine," I said, looking back at the police who were busy pushing people in the opposite direction, "But then we have to go," I told him.

As Ricky danced out his 'four more minutes,' i.e., about 45 seconds, I noticed something small and hot pink, glowing at my feet. Normally you can't see things on the floor of a club, but with the house lights on and people scattering away from the cops, all was revealed. I knelt down to try and focus on this magical little item on the concrete, but my vision was tripled over, turning the item into threes and then those threes into three more. Whatever it was, it matched my outfit. I *had* to have it. I picked it up and shoved it in my pocket.

"Girl, what are you doing?" Magically, Melanie was now squatting next to me with a concerned look on her face, "Yo. The cops are arresting people. We need to go," she said.

"Oh thank God for you. Ricky might actually listen to you," I said nodding toward Ricky, who was, predictably, still dancing in the mirror.

"Oh my fucking God, Ricky, it is TIME TO GO," Melanie said sternly.

She stood and pulled on one of Ricky's arms, hard.

"Go, just go, I'll get him out of here. Save yourself girl," she said, gently pushing me away.

The cops were busy harassing other people, mostly the few people who looked over 25. My guess was they wanted the dealers and their drugs and a payoff from the club owners. No one seemed concerned about the underage kids spilling out onto the streets of South East like a ripped-open pack of Skittles.

I snuck out through a side door and into the morning light. The sun was up, the winter clouds thick.

"Auriane!" I heard Frances yell my name from behind me.

She ran up and jumped on top of me, piggy back, hugging me so hard it hurt, her nails scraping into my shoulders.

"We found you!" She dug deeper, her white platform sneakers kicking me in my sides like you would a horse.

Frances was tiny, maybe weighed 85 pounds soaking wet, but she was an aggressive little thing when she was on drugs. I pried her fingers from around my neck, put her down and faced her. Her eyes rolled around in her head like gumballs as she chewed violently on a bent up plastic straw.

"So where are we going?" she asked excitedly.

Angel and Chelsea were a few feet behind her, walking with intention away from the cops and the club.

"Yo, we need to go," Chelsea said.

"Yeah, but where are we going?" I asked.

"Jacob said we're all meeting at the McDonald's. To figure out where to after party," Angel said.

"Okay then, there we have it," I said as we walked back to the car, which—thank the Party Gods--had not been towed.

We squeezed into Chelsea's four speed Honda and put-putted over a few blocks to the nearby McDonalds. Ravers were huddled in small groups throughout the parking lot. We were a sharp contrast with the few remaining bums staggering around, and the morning breakfast customers—commuters coming off of 395, on their way to work at the Capitol. I reached into my pocket to see if I had any money. I was oddly in the mood for a Bacon Egg and Cheese.

"We need to get orange juice," Frances said with gusto as she kicked the back of my seat.

"I think I have some cash left," I told her, playing with something unusual, small and smooth in my pocket. I placed it in my palm and examined it. It was still pink. But in the morning light, this was no enchanted object. It was a little baggie used for drugs. I squinted. My vision was still off from the Acid. I pried open the bag and shook its contents out into my hand. Four small, speckled pills, pressed with a stamp of three, tiered triangles scattered over my skin.

"Oh shit," I said.

"What is it?" Frances squirmed and shot forward from the backseat, into the small space between Chelsea and I in the front.

I showed her the pills.

"Mitsubishis!" She reached out to take one immediately.

Angel followed suit and I offered my hand to Chelsea. The idea of getting McDonald's food was suddenly lost on us.

"Look," I pointed at Jacob, standing taller than most of our friends in the parking lot. He and Matt were getting into a boxy silver Buick with Ben, Melanie and Ricky. His sugar daddy was in the driver's seat. He smiled and waved for us to follow them.

Chelsea placed her pill in her mouth and swallowed it with a gulp of blue Gatorade, offering each of us a swig. She passed the bottle to Angel and Frances in the back seat. They chugged down a pill a piece. Chelsea started the car.

"Guys, STOP!" Frances shrieked out.

We jerked forward to a halt. Chelsea had slammed on the brakes, causing the car to stall. Angel, Chelsea and I looked at Frances.

"Three girls...." Frances said in a low tone.

We stared and waited through a dramatic pause. Frances' eyes rolled back in her head and her jaw quivered.

"Misbehaving..." she said, louder now, and smiled like a jackal.

Frances started to laugh. The rest of us joined in.

"Jesus Christ, you're wasted tonight," Chelsea said, turning her attention back to the steering wheel.

"Yeah dude, there's four of us," Angel pointed out, "I'm not an actual boy, you know," she effeminately ran her fingers through her short platinum hair, buzzed to almost the scalp on both sides.

I looked at the three girls, eyes wide, sweaty and covered in glitter. I placed the last pill on my tongue and chased it down with a swig of the Gatorade.

"I fuckin' love you guys so much," I said.

Chelsea restarted the car, the mixtape in her cassette deck coming to life.

'It's a fine day...People open windows...' the song started.

Morning sun peeked out from behind the clouds. We turned out of the parking lot just in time to follow our friends; Our own fucked up little caravan, on our way to the next party.

***

Just as there are different kinds of music, people, parties...there are different kinds of ghosts. A Residual Haunting, like the one at Capitol Riverfront, is created when an energy so powerful creates an impression on the atmosphere where it was released. This impression is usually intensely traumatic or one of joy—an extreme emotion. The same way a DJ can put a track on wax, this energy records itself, to be played, over and over again.

Visitors to the Capitol Riverfront have reported hearing the thumping of distant bass and feeling their jaws chatter mysteriously in the night. There have been multiple reports of residents feeling a girls' fingernails unexpectedly claw into their backs for a piggy back ride, as they walk to their cars each morning.

"That happened to me," former Mayor Adrian Fenty told DC ghost-hunter podcast, Boo! in 2007, "It was at the ribbon cutting, I almost cut my fingers off, I was so scared," he said, "She whispered 'Misbehaving,' very mischievously into my ear, and then she was gone," he added.

People patronizing the local shops often complain that they have brief hallucinations. Complaints of seeing shifting or melting faces of retail employees has turned the shopping district from ideal to spooky.

Recently, two young newlyweds, Brett and Mara Ackridge, reported seeing an apparition in the bathroom mirror of their condo, in the neighborhood's beautiful Envy building.

"It's pretty terrifying," Mara Ackridge told the DC City Paper, "This man, he's so pale and dripping sweat. He just dances and dances, but he never turns to face you."

"It's like he's watching himself. He dances there for four minutes, exactly. I timed it. Then he disappears. We see him almost every weekend," Brett Ackridge added.

The ghost stories spilling from the Capitol Riverfront don't end there. Mysteriously long lines around condo buildings and phantom police raids that disappear in the blink of an eye are just a few more examples.

In the late 90s, there was an ethereal impression recorded on the streets of South East DC. That impression—although intense enough to remain today--was not one of trauma or sorrow. That impression was one of togetherness and resilience. That impression was, and is, one of youthful joy in the face of adversity. My friends made that impression.

The ghosts that inhabit South East are not those of the lost souls ducking behind cars, or begging for cash on the street. The ghosts haunting Capitol Riverfront today are Ravers. And yeah, sure. We *scare* people. But what did you expect? We're teenagers.

10

The Nashville Shitter

Working in Downtown Nashville, you meet a lot of characters. The streets are lined with bars blasting live music, and people come from all over to get in on the Honky-Tonk fun. I worked Downtown's busy upper Broadway from 2012 to 2016. The story of The Nashville Shitter, since I was working at Layla's Bluegrass Inn at the time, would have happened around 2014. Let's take a magical trip back to a simpler time. The year when Pharrell wore that ridiculous hat. The year when every child in the country would not Let it Go. And my personal fave, the year when gay people could finally get legally married. Barack Obama was president, Nashville was booming (but not so hard that it sucked) and life was gravy. But this is not a story about gravy. This is a story about poop.

There is a hierarchy of bars in Nashville. There's the Gulch and Midtown and East Nashville bars, all of those are really on the same tier. They're neighborhood bars. They're tough to get into (as a bartender, not as a patron), the money is really good, and they lack the cheesy, touristy factor of the downtown bars. There's Downtown 2nd street bars, those are kind of ratchet and have more of a nightclub vibe instead of the old, honky-tonk vibe. You can still make good money there, but there are slow nights and the off season is a struggle. The downtown bars on upper Broadway, though, are *money*. I'm talking expensive call-girl money. I am not joking when I tell you that at the height of my bar career on Upper Broadway I sometimes made well over $1,000. On my best nights I made more than 2. I know. Opening beers. It's ridiculous.

Because the money is so good, it's very competitive. Also, with the good shifts, you have to accept the bad. Most bartenders awarded Friday and Saturday nights also have to take some crap day shift. When I was hired at Layla's, my crappy day shift was Wednesday.

Layla's was really funny during the day because we offered $1 PBRs. This means that we got a lot of homeless regulars. More often than not, my Wednesday day shifts were five or six toothless bums, grumbling weird things about marrying me over the bar, while a few tourists gawked at the scene. In the foreground Amanda Taylor and her momma Paula Jo played live country classics for us all.

I had a favorite homeless regular named Johnny. Johnny was the best. He would stand out front, barking to the passers-by about how Layla's had the best bartender in town. He'd yell about our ice cold PBRs and actually bring in a decent amount of business, all in exchange for two or three PBRs for himself. Johnny ran a coffee kiosk and sold the local homeless paper, the Contributor. Johnny cried when Amanda Taylor would sing Coat of Many Colors by Dolly Parton, and every time would make up a different tall tale to explain his tears. Oh yeah, Johnny lied a lot. He was like the bar's own Uncle Remus, always making up something crazy, but it only made him more lovable. One time, right after taking a shot of whiskey with me, Johnny told me he had just had a liver transplant only the night before. So yeah, Johnny lied about stuff. But that's part of his charm.

On Wednesdays, I got off work at 6 and was replaced by Jake. Jake was tall and handsome with a Boston accent. He was no nonsense, but a nice guy, and had worked at Layla's for years. I liked him. Jake seemed to enjoy his job at Laylas, but lately one thing had really been dragging him down: Jake kept having *incidents* with The Nashville Shitter.

The Nashville Shitter was a ghost, a legend, a real sick-o. He or she would sneak from bar to bar, smearing feces on barstools every few months. When Jake would come in to start his shift, he'd go red with fury when he realized there had been another poop attack.

"Someone smeared shit! Again! Fucking goddammit! What kind of animal!" He would yell, "Who did this? Someone had to see who did this," he'd continue, frustrated with me.

But I didn't see anything. I really didn't.

After three Shitter instances on my Wednesday shift, with Jake growing more and more furious with me, I knew I had to solve this. I had to find out who the Shitter was. I didn't suspect any of my regulars, but they weren't to be ignored. People can do crazy things, especially when they're dealing with the trauma of homelessness and they're on their 7th PBR.

First up was Johnny. I knew it wasn't him, but Johnny

might know something I didn't. I inquired if he had seen anything suspicious, or heard of any other attacks.

"Oh yeah, Legends got hit, so did The Wheel, in fact, it was when Amanda was playing. I don't know about Legends, but she plays there sometimes, too." His voice was gruff and throaty.

"So maybe he's following Amanda," I said, rubbing my chin, "Very interesting."

Next up was Cecil. Cecil was a short, pink little man with no front teeth who ran a shoe shine business on the front stoop of the bar. He'd sit, with his box, his brush and his shoe polish and make a few bucks each morning.

"Cecil, you ever had to clean a shoe with shit on it?" I asked, leaning over the bar-top, toward him, "Like, not dog shit, like *human shit.*"

"What the fuck?!" Cecil looked shocked which was surprising because Cecil had a disgusting sense of humor. It seemed clear though that, no, Cecil hadn't noticed any human poop on the shoes of his recent customers.

I asked Amanda if she had any particularly odd fans that she thought might be following her from bar to bar.

"Uhh, all of them?" Amanda was a smoking hot blonde and played all over Downtown. Point taken.

This was getting nowhere.

"Excuse me, young lady," I heard a deep voice behind me at the bar. I turned to see a tall man, with dark, late-Elvis dyed black hair, sideburns and all.

"Hi there," I recognized the man. I had waited on him a few times, but didn't know his name.

"PBR me, ASAP," he sat down and put a single dollar bill on the bar.

Even my homeless guys tipped me *something*. Eye. Roll.

I gave the man his beer and went back to talk to Johnny. We were chatting, going over the list of suspects, when the man started talking, to no one, loudly.

"You know that Taylor Swift really owes me a lot of thank-yous," his booming voice was impossible to ignore, "I wrote every damn one of those hits she keeps crankin' out and what appreciation do I get? Nothin', that's what."

This guy was clearly drunk and crazier than Hell. I egged him on.

"What a total bitch! Did she at least pay you for them?"

"She stole them. I coulda' been rich and famous but here I am. Dollar beer and all," he lamented.

I looked over to Johnny and made an '*Are you getting this*?' face. Johnny twirled his pointer finger around in a circle by his temple and mouthed '*Crazy as fuck*' my way.

"You ever hear a song that...that ...well it just makes you wanna' *do somethin'* to someone?" The sideburned man asked creepily.

I looked nervously at the man. He had one hand on the bar, wrapped around his beer. His other arm was tucked behind him and under his butt. He was sitting on his hand. This was weird, and given my current investigation, a cause for concern. I was peripherally a little worried for Taylor Swift's safety, due to the whole '*do something*' comment.

Amanda Taylor ended her rendition of Dolly Parton's I

Will Always Love You softly on stage and the band now burst into a lively rendition of Mama Tried by Merle Haggard.

At this, the strange man sprung up from his seat to dance. It was then that I saw it, he'd had his hand down his pants while he was sitting on it. He pulled his hand out and started to dance like there was nothing strange going on at all.

"Johnny," I whispered in the opposite direction, nodding my head toward the man, "Johnny!!" He looked up from his beer, "Johnny, I think that's The Shitter!"

The man was dancing wildly, and every few moments would stop to touch his butt. Like, he'd pause and kind of wiggle, and press his hand into his crack, but over the pants. He danced this way through the entire song, and by the end, both Johnny and I were convinced: We had found The Nashville Shitter and it was time to shut him down.

At the end of the song, The Shitter excused himself to use the men's room. I turned to Johnny, still whispering.

"Johnny, that's definitely him. You gotta' go in there and stop him before he comes out and smears his shit on everything!"

"You got it toots," Johnny said, polishing off the last of his free PBR and nodding his head, "I'll gladly take care of this problem for one, ice cold PBR."

Johnny disappeared to the men's room, and returned five minutes later with a huge grin on his face.

"You won't need to worry about seeing The Nashville Shitter again," he assured me as I cracked his beer.

"What did you say to him?" I asked.

"I just told him. I said, 'Lookit man. The bartender knows

you've been smearing your shit all over the bar. She knows you're The Nashville Shitter. She doesn't want to make a scene but you're fuckin' banned from here on out, you understand me? Now finish up and don't you even think about smearing your shit on anything on your way out.' Nasty sonofabitch."

Just as he finished his sentence, I heard the click of the backdoor opening. I turned quickly and caught a glimpse of the Shitter, fleeing from the men's room and out to the alley. I ran over to the men's bathroom and peeped inside. I scanned the walls and toilet seat with my eyes. No trace of any poop! We had stopped The Nashville Shitter!

"Goddammit Johnny, you are the best," I mixed up two blueberry bombs and passed one his way, "Cheers, babe. You earned it."

6 o'clock rolled around and Jake came in as scheduled.

"Jake!" Johnny usually hated Jake because he wasn't a cute chick and didn't give him free beer, but today Johnny was proud and wanted to share.

"Hey Johnny," Jake said unenthusiastically, approaching the entrance of the bar.

I was busy counting down the cash in my register, but listened as Johnny told Jake the good news.

"We caught The Shitter today and we tossed his ass out! He's gone, we caught the bastard!"

"Who was it? Wait, really? Did he shit on anything?" Jake started to look at the barstools lining the bar, the usual spot for The Shitter to strike.

"Nope, Auriane caught on to him early on account of him

digging all in his butt on the dancefloor. And I kicked his ass out. Told him 'you better not shit on this bar no more you sick sonofabitch.' So, you're welcome," Johnny said, beer suds in his moustache.

"Then what the fuck is this?" Jake asked, his skin reddening, "There's fuckin shit all over this!" Jake shouted.

He pointed at the stool where the Shitter had sat. There was a large smear of poop around the side of the stool.

Johnny looked over to see. I just kept counting money, trying not to bust out laughing at the sheer insanity of it all.

"Oh, well...we caught the bastard," Johnny said in his gravelly voice, "And The Nashville Shitter won't be shittin' at Layla's no more."

FIN.
For information on upcoming events and giveaways,
email me at Aurianederudder@gmail.com and get on my list!

www.ingramcontent.com/pod-product-compliance
Lightning Source LLC
Chambersburg PA
CBHW070623120726
47909CB00004B/1295